EMPOWERING EAL LEARNERS IN SECONDARY SCHOOLS

One in five students are identified as speaking English as an Additional Language (EAL) and all teachers are highly likely to be teaching multilingual students in their classrooms. As our schools become more culturally and linguistically diverse, they must respond to the needs of the students in front of them, and this book provides a range of strategies and resources to ensure teaching is adaptive and responsive so that all learners thrive and fulfil their academic potential.

At the heart of the book is developing an understanding of how languages are acquired and an awareness that all students, regardless of their current English language proficiency, need to be offered a challenging and supportive environment. Chapters offer:

- High-yielding, practical approaches and strategies to ensure that students are able to access content-appropriate lessons and simultaneously develop their language.
- A plethora of resources and step-by-step examples, showcasing how explicit vocabulary and grammar learning can be context-based for the benefit of all learners.

Each teacher is positioned as a language teacher, with the responsibility of planning sessions where language is not perceived as an add-on, but as an integral and pivotal part. This book will empower you as an educator and ensure that your classroom is a language-aware and stimulating environment for your students. It will be essential reading for all secondary school educators and teaching assistants who support EAL students in mainstream lessons and are responsible for producing resources and implementing classroom strategies.

Joanna Kolota is Curriculum Leader: Multilingual Learners at Trinity Academy Leeds, UK. She has worked in extremely diverse settings supporting multilingual students in primary, secondary and tertiary education for over ten years. She also regularly delivers training to whole school staff and more bespoke department training, focusing on embedding best pedagogy to advance EAL learners' linguistic development.

EMPOWERING EAL LEARNERS IN SECONDARY SCHOOLS

A Practical Resource to Support the Language Development of Multilingual Learners

Joanna Kolota

LONDON AND NEW YORK

Designed cover image: © Getty images

First published 2024
by Routledge
4 Park Square, Milton Park, Abingdon, Oxon OX14 4RN

and by Routledge
605 Third Avenue, New York, NY 10158

Routledge is an imprint of the Taylor & Francis Group, an informa business

© 2024 Joanna Kolota

The right of Joanna Kolota to be identified as author of this work has been asserted in accordance with sections 77 and 78 of the Copyright, Designs and Patents Act 1988.

All rights reserved. No part of this book may be reprinted or reproduced or utilised in any form or by any electronic, mechanical, or other means, now known or hereafter invented, including photocopying and recording, or in any information storage or retrieval system, without permission in writing from the publishers.

Trademark notice: Product or corporate names may be trademarks or registered trademarks, and are used only for identification and explanation without intent to infringe.

British Library Cataloguing-in-Publication Data
A catalogue record for this book is available from the British Library

Library of Congress Cataloging-in-Publication Data
Names: Kolota, Joanna, author.
Title: Empowering EAL learners in secondary schools : a practical resource to support the language development of multilingual learners / Joanna Kolota.
Description: Abingdon, Oxon ; New York, NY : Routledge, 2024. | Includes bibliographical references and index.
Identifiers: LCCN 2023059200 (print) | LCCN 2023059201 (ebook) | ISBN 9781032479781 (hardback) | ISBN 9781032479798 (paperback) | ISBN 9781003386810 (ebook)
Subjects: LCSH: Language arts (Secondary)--Correlation with content subjects. | Multilingual persons--Education (Secondary) | English-medium instruction. | English language--Study and teaching (Secondary)--Foreign speakers.
Classification: LCC P53.293 .K65 2024 (print) | LCC P53.293 (ebook) | DDC 428.0071/2--dc23/eng/20240404
LC record available at https://lccn.loc.gov/2023059200
LC ebook record available at https://lccn.loc.gov/2023059201

ISBN: 978-1-032-47978-1 (hbk)
ISBN: 978-1-032-47979-8 (pbk)
ISBN: 978-1-003-38681-0 (ebk)

DOI: 10.4324/9781003386810

Typeset in Interstate
by Deanta Global Publishing Services, Chennai, India

CONTENTS

List of figures	*vii*

1 Unlocking the diversity of EAL students: Bridging languages and classrooms   **1**
English as an Additional Language: what does it mean?   *1*
What is 'language'?   *4*
Who are EAL learners?   *6*
Who and how teaches EAL learners?   *10*
Theories about first language acquisition   *14*
Theories about second language acquisition   *16*
What is good practice for EAL learners?   *18*
How long does it take to learn a new language?   *19*
The perfect match: content and language   *24*
References   *26*

2 Building a strong foundation: Vocabulary development in subject lessons   **28**
Why is vocabulary teaching important?   *28*
1, 2, 3, words   *30*
Tier 1: the (in)frequent words   *33*
Tier 2: the universal words   *37*
Tier 3: the domain-specific words   *40*
All words are important   *44*
Beyond single words   *47*
Summary   *52*
References   *53*

3 The power of a single sentence   **54**
Relationships within a single sentence   *54*
Speaking in full sentences   *57*
Teaching sentence writing explicitly   *59*
Summary   *62*
References   *63*

4 Navigating the worlds of words: Reading skills and EAL learners   **64**
Graphic organisers for reading   *66*
Summary   *70*
Cohesion: what keeps the text together?   *71*
Summary   *72*

Summary	76
References	77

5 Striking the balance: Simplification vs easification for EAL learners — 78
What's the difference? — 79
Non-fiction texts — 80
Alternative versions of non-fiction texts — 83
Fiction texts — 87
Easification devices for literary texts — 88
Summary — 91
References — 93

6 'One to bring them all': The multifaceted worlds of writing for EAL students — 94
Why might writing be challenging for EAL learners? — 95
Substitution tables — 96
Summary — 99
Graphic organisers — 100
Summary — 103
Parallel writing — 104
Parallel sentences — 104
Parallel paragraphs — 105
Summary — 109
Dictation activities — 110
Sentence dictation — 110
Transformation dictation — 113
Dictogloss — 115
Summary — 119
Routines and habits aka sentence starters and frames — 121
Summary — 125
References — 125

Conclusion — 127

Index — 129

FIGURES

1.1	Profiles of multilingual learners can be shared with teaching and support staff prior to the students' first day in mainstream lessons. These profiles offer concise information about the students' backgrounds, enabling the creation of a supportive and inclusive environment, as well as effective support	6
1.2	At Trinity Academy Leeds, students take pride in their multilingualism. They understand the power and significance of different languages in their lives	9
1.3	English Language Teaching encompasses many different contexts in which the English language is taught. There are some overlaps and distinctive features between these approaches	12
1.4	English language proficiency levels are the strongest indicators of a multilingual learner's academic attainment	20
1.5	Conversational and academic language proficiency are both important to multilingual learners' language development. Adapted from: Cummins, J. 2021. *Rethinking the Education of Multilingual Learners*. Bristol: Multilingual Matters	23
1.6	What we teach should form the core of our lessons, while how we teach it must be a proactive response to the students in our classroom	25
2.1	Vocabulary is learned more effectively when introduced and practised in meaningful contexts rather than in isolation or as long lists of words	30
2.2	There are several factors teachers can consider when choosing vocabulary to be studied and focused on during lessons	31
2.3	Focusing students' attention on root words as well as their affixes will help students notice patterns and increase their awareness of how some words are created and connect	32
2.4	Identifying key vocabulary for a unit or a series of lessons ensures that teachers can decide how each word and phrase is going to be practised by students through various activities	33
2.5	Word cards with key words, translation, pictures and definitions	35
2.6	Word cards with key words, translation, pictures, definitions and example sentences	35
2.7	Students should be encouraged to produce their own word cards and practise recalling key information independently	36
2.8	Visuals may help establish the meaning of some concrete words. Created by Gan Khoon Lay from Noun Project	37

2.9	The five-step model to introduce and practise key academic vocabulary	39
2.10	The Frayer model allows the practice of key vocabulary related to concepts studied in a variety of subjects	42
2.11	The Frayer model is easily adaptable; further study of key vocabulary, its roots, affixes and etymology can be added to deepen students' understanding of key words	43
2.12	Identifying key vocabulary in each tier might support teachers with a systematic and structured approach to vocabulary teaching in mainstream lessons	44
2.13	Keeping notes of key words and phrases can encourage students to look for connections between the words they already know and allows them to create a personalised record of important vocabulary	46
2.14	One of the activities focusing on students' vocabulary development might be matching collocations and their explanations	49
2.15	Translating phrases and expressions, such as idioms or collocations, allows students to use all their linguistic repertoire to draw connections between the languages or notice the differences	50
3.1	Chunking sentences into smaller units can enhance comprehension by breaking down complex information into more manageable, digestible segments, making it easier for students to grasp and process the content	56
3.2	This process of chunking sentences can be initially modelled by the teacher, enabling students to subsequently practise it independently	56
3.3	Students can learn how to systematically divide a sentence into distinct, digestible segments, aiding their comprehension	57
3.4	Students may be asked to recall key information and organise it in a table, before writing full sentences	60
3.5	Modelling sentences is an effective technique and offers students easy steps to follow	60
3.6	Using consistent patterns will allow for students' increased independence	61
3.7	Modelling how to write sentences can employ a certain level of flexibility	62
4.1	Graphic organisers can prove highly effective in facilitating comprehension	67
4.2	Teachers can effectively demonstrate the thinking process behind completing a graphic organiser, providing students with a valuable model	68
4.3	In addition to illustrating the relationships between key figures, graphic organisers in reading can also depict the sequence of events	69
4.4	Using visuals aids supports multilingual learners in establishing and reinforcing the meaning of new words	74
4.5	Consistent use of the same pictures supports multilingual learners in memorising the words more effectively	75
5.1	Labelling and colour-coding diagrams and pictures contributes to creating meaningful input	81
5.2	Graphic organisers assist students in breaking down longer texts into manageable sections while preserving the integrity of the ideas and writing style	83
5.3	The use of text, pictures and colours enhances the meaning of passages	85
5.4	Alternative ways of presenting the same content might allow for better comprehension	85
5.5	Modification can be used to present longer passages	86

5.6	Improving student comprehension can be facilitated by offering concise summaries and connecting them to students' personal experiences	89
5.7	Comprehending cultural references and nuances is crucial for understanding texts originating from diverse cultures	89
5.8	A number of easification devices applied to a literary text	90
6.1	A three-column substitution table for assessing students' knowledge and emphasising the use of past tense	97
6.2	Substitution tables give the flexibility to include visuals	97
6.3	Substitution tables should highlight key grammatical points for effective language learning	97
6.4	Substitution tables allow for a great level of flexibility	98
6.5	Thanks to substitution tables we can focus on key grammatical or lexical items	99
6.6	Graphic organisers help visually structure and organise ideas, enhancing clarity and coherence in the written work	101
6.7	Scaffolding and language planning are equally as crucial as content planning	102
6.8	Content and language should be equally important when designing materials for EAL learners	103
6.9	The essential information required for the writing task may either be provided in advance or used as a retrieval exercise	105
6.10	During the preparation stage, students could be provided with the key information necessary to complete the written task	106
6.11	As part of a preparation and retrieval task, students could be prompted to independently recall essential information	107
6.12	The exemplar text explicitly models what should be included in the response and how it should be composed linguistically	108
6.13	A retrieval task preparing students for the main writing stage	108
6.14	A language scaffold in the form of a writing frame could be provided. Students may also wish to refer to the model introduced earlier	109
6.15	Similar information can be conveyed using different grammatical structures	111
6.16	Incorporating visuals aids supports multilingual learners in grasping the meaning of important words and understanding the sequences of a process	112
6.17	A gap-filling exercise encourages students to recall essential information and practise transforming grammatical structures	114
6.18	A completed example of a gap-filling exercise	114
6.19	Dictogloss can be easily adapted to support learners at different levels	115
6.20	Thanks to dictogloss we can focus on key grammatical items	116
6.21	Dictogloss can be used with students at all levels of English language acquisition	117
6.22	It is beneficial if particular grammatical structures are highlighted during dictation tasks	118
6.23	Using a template with visuals can assist students in comprehending and completing each step of a dictation activity	120
6.24	Sentence starters are invaluable tools for EAL learners as they provide a foundation for expressing their thoughts and ideas effectively in English	122
6.25	Combining the content and linguistic components of lessons using sentence starters creates a supportive environment for EAL learners	124
6.26	Speaking and writing frames allow for the adjustment of linguistic complexity	124

1 Unlocking the diversity of EAL students
Bridging languages and classrooms

It is a Friday morning and you are about to welcome a class of 24 Year 7 students. Today's geography lesson continues the water unit, with a focus on the Nile River, its significance and contemporary uses for transportation. As you stand at the classroom threshold, you notice an unfamiliar student accompanied by a staff member. Then you recall that a new student is joining your group today. Adam started earlier this week and completed a brief induction programme, during which he was introduced to the school, its routines, expectations, some of the lessons, teachers and students. He also completed a couple of initial informal assessments. The information and the student's profile you received yesterday indicated that Adam is an English as an Additional Language (EAL) student in the early stages of developing his English language competencies.

English as an Additional Language: what does it mean?

From a statistical perspective, Adam is set to become the fifth **English as an Additional Language** (EAL) or **multilingual student** to join your class. These two terms, EAL and multilingual, are going to be interchangeably used throughout this book as there is some overlap between them. The former is the official one used by the Department of Education in England. The latter, however, is much more inclusive and focuses all on languages, not just English. In other countries, terms such as **EL** (English Learners) or **ESL** (English as a Second Language) are also used. If you are a teacher in England or, in fact, many other countries worldwide, it is highly likely that at some point in your professional career, you will have both the privilege and the responsibility of teaching and supporting learners who use languages other than English. EAL learners typically attend **mainstream schools** where English predominantly serves as the **primary language of instruction** in subject classrooms and throughout the broader school community. In 2023 a report commissioned by the Department for Education stated that 20.2% of all students in English schools and nurseries were categorised as pupils who use English as an additional language (United Kingdom Statistics Authority, 2023). It also points out that there has been an increase in the number of EAL students and this trend is expected to prevail.

At this point, it is essential to consider the precise definition of an EAL learner, as provided by the Department of Education: 'A pupil is recorded as having English as an additional language if she/he is exposed to a language at home that is known or believed to be other than English. It is not a measure of English language proficiency or a good proxy for recent immigration' (DfE, 2020).

It is worth noting that the phrase 'is exposed to a language' appears to lack specificity, leaving room for various interpretations. It fails to clarify the nature and extent of exposure to the first language (L1), whether it involves passive listening or active engagement in using the language. Furthermore, it omits a clear definition of what is meant by 'language'. As we will explore in this chapter, understanding the nuanced concept of 'language' is pivotal to gaining a comprehensive understanding of the diverse characteristics of students who use English as an Additional Language. Moreover, the definition underscores the wide spectrum and the diversity of linguistic repertoire and competencies that students may possess. This spectrum ranges from a high level of competence in a given language to a more loosely defined connection and exposure to a different language.

The language identities of multilingual learners are perpetually fluid, dynamic and evolving. This encompasses their language development, increased usage, as well as the gradual, often unconscious and sometimes deliberate fading of languages from their lives. Typically, when we reference an individual using a language, we consider their ability to communicate through spoken and written words, their comprehension of spoken language and their capacity to convey messages in written form. For many multilingual learners, this accurately describes their competence in their first language. This description predominantly fits students who attended schools in their home countries, recently moved to England and experienced minimal disruptions in their formal education. They have typically achieved, or at the very least established, fundamental literacy skills in their first languages. These skills extend across all four language domains: speaking, listening, reading and writing. Many of these students may have moved to England for various reasons, such as economic, political or educational motivations. They may also be children who have spent a significant portion of their lives in England, with parents and families actively supporting their first language education. This support may involve teaching them language skills in their L1 or investing in their education by enrolling them in supplementary schools. These schools are often offered free of charge and are affiliated with places of worship or local community centres.

Many children, whether born in England or having moved here as babies or toddlers, have achieved literacy in both their first language (L1) and English, rendering them **biliterate**. This phenomenon can also be described as **additive biliteracy**, where a student acquires and utilises a second language (L2) without diminishing or subtracting from their proficiency in their first language. In simpler terms, when someone becomes an additive biliterate individual, their proficiency in their first language remains intact and is not compromised as they acquire and use a second language. These students can effectively operate in and across both languages, maintaining similar levels of competence.

Key characteristics of additive biliteracy include:

- **positive language transfer:** the skills and knowledge acquired in L1 can support the acquisition of the second language. There is a positive transfer of language skills and cognitive benefits from knowing two languages.
- **maintaining and developing L1:** individuals who are additively biliterate continue to develop and use their first language alongside the second language. This often involves maintaining their cultural identity and connections to their community.
- **bicultural identity:** those who use their first and second languages they have acquired, usually have a stronger connection to both the culture and heritage.
- **balanced proficiency:** students can achieve a high level of proficiency in both their first language and their second language. This balanced proficiency enables them to navigate various linguistic and cultural contexts effectively.

Students who have not developed the ability to read or write proficiently in their first language or can only do so at a basic level are typically referred to as **bilingual learners**. In contrast to biliteracy, **bilingualism** primarily emphasises spoken communication. However, many of the characteristics mentioned earlier for biliteracy also apply to bilingualism. These students tend to have well-developed speaking and listening skills, particularly in everyday, habitual and routine situations. Their capacity to engage in academic discussions largely depends on their previous educational background. If they attended schools where other languages were used, they would likely possess the ability to read, write and discuss various school-related topics. For many bilingual learners, the proficiency of their reading and writing skills tends to decline quickly and significantly, as these skills are often not regularly practised at higher levels, particularly in young children. Additionally, some students are at risk of losing or weakening their abilities in their first languages as they acquire and use a second language. This scenario is known as **subtractive bilingualism** because the use of a second language comes at the expense of the first language. Subtractive bilingualism frequently occurs when there is strong parental, societal or educational pressure to assimilate into the culture and language of the dominant group, often resulting in the abandonment or devaluation of one's first language.

Key characteristics of subtractive bilingualism include:

- **loss of proficiency:** in subtractive bilingualism, the first language may gradually lose proficiency as more emphasis is placed on the second language. This can lead to decreased fluency, vocabulary and literacy skills in the first language.
- **cultural disconnection:** students may experience disconnect from their cultural heritage and community as they adopt the dominant culture and language, often at the expense of their heritage culture.
- **identity challenges:** some individuals might struggle to grapple with their dual linguistic and cultural identity if one of them is deliberately removed.
- **language shift:** in some cases of subtractive bilingualism, individuals may completely shift to the second language as their primary means of communication, abandoning their first languages altogether.

Subtractive bilingualism is frequently linked to policies or situations that discourage the use of minority languages while promoting assimilation into the dominant culture. This can have detrimental effects on individuals and communities, potentially leading to the loss of cultural diversity and the erosion of linguistic heritage.

The phrase 'exposed to other languages', therefore, holds particular significance as it clarifies that being classified as an EAL learner does not necessarily mean fluency in speaking another language, complete understanding of all spoken interactions, the ability to compose written messages or reading various texts. The definition unequivocally states that it encompasses a linguistically **diverse group of students**. Among them, some may have been raised as **simultaneous bilinguals**, meaning they acquired and developed proficiency in two languages from birth or early childhood. They have been exposed to both languages in their daily environment and have learnt to use them interchangeably. This can occur in various ways, such as when parents speak different languages at home or when a child grows up in a multicultural community. Simultaneous bilingualism often leads to a high level of fluency in both languages, often with proficiency in pronunciation and grammar. Conversely, in **sequential bilingualism**, individuals acquire proficiency in a second language after already developing skills in their first language. This typically occurs when someone learns a second language, as Adam will, later in life, perhaps through formal education or by moving to a different region or country where the second language is spoken. However, it is important to acknowledge that language is far more than just words.

What is 'language'?

Language, from a linguistic perspective, is **a system of communication** that utilises symbols, like words, and rules, such as grammar, to enable humans to convey and comprehend meaning. This encompasses various fields of study, including phonetics and phonology (the examination of speech sounds, their production and patterns in language), morphology (the analysis of word structure), syntax (the exploration of sentence structure), semantics (the investigation of meaning in language) and pragmatics (the study of how language is employed in context, including the interpretation of implied meaning, politeness and more). The preceding paragraphs have examined multilingual learners from a linguistic viewpoint. They classified students as either EAL or non-EAL based on the assumption that these students can, to varying degrees, communicate and understand a language other than English.

Language, however, is a complex and multifaceted concept and its definition can vary depending on the field of study. Consequently, our group of EAL learners may be more extensive and diverse than we initially perceive. From an anthropological perspective, language is viewed through a cultural and social lens. In this context, language serves as **a cultural tool** that mirrors and influences the beliefs, values and practices of a particular group of people. Anthropologists investigate how language is employed in different societies. For instance, understanding even a few words used in specific ceremonies, rituals, or to name clothing or food can be crucial for grasping the cultural significance of these events.

Language is also closely **tied to individual and group identities**. In a multilingual community or household, the choice of language or dialect can convey group identity or express affection or irritation. In these scenarios, individuals may not be able to speak the language fluently or fully comprehend interactions among proficient speakers. Nevertheless, it cannot be denied that they are indeed 'exposed' to language. Consider, for instance, children born in the UK who primarily speak English but regularly interact with users of other languages, such as relatives or friends. In such cases, they may be considered as EAL students.

These students may also be referred to as individuals who use '**heritage languages**'. In a broader sense of this term, speakers of heritage languages may not necessarily speak or fully understand their family's or community's language, but there exists a connection between their linguistic and cultural backgrounds (Polinsky and Kagan, 2007). In a more comprehensive definition, heritage speakers are identified as individuals who grow up in a community or household where a language other than the dominant language of the region or country is spoken. These individuals acquire a certain level of proficiency in the heritage language primarily through exposure within their family or community, as opposed to formal education. Heritage speakers are often bilingual or multilingual and typically have a personal connection or cultural heritage tied to the language they acquire as heritage speakers. There are significant overlaps between the characteristics of English as an Additional Language students and heritage language speakers, and these terms may be used interchangeably to underscore the linguistic diversity and complexity of these learners. The acronym 'EAL' is most commonly used in England to describe students who speak other languages, while the phrase 'heritage languages' is mainly employed to describe the GCSE exams that students can take if they are biliterate. In recent years, there has been a deliberate shift towards using the term 'multilingual' in England and other countries, rather than 'EAL', as the latter places English at the forefront and fails to acknowledge the linguistic repertoire of all students (Cummins, 2021; Snyder and Fenner, 2021). Another key distinction is that 'EAL' is specifically related to English language acquisition in an educational context, whereas 'multilingualism' recognises, affirms and nurtures all individuals' languages.

Given the complexity of the concept of language, it does not always have to equate solely to words and communication; it might also encompass growing up and being 'exposed' to the cultural and more tangible aspects of it, such as traditions, clothing, food or religious observances. There are various angles from which language is studied, analysed and defined. This includes neurolinguistics, which investigates the neural and biological basis of language; psychology, which focuses on how language influences human behaviour, serving as a tool for communication and a means of understanding emotions and cognition; and literary studies, where language is celebrated as a creative and abstract medium. However we decide to approach and define languages, they all serve as bridges to understanding and personal growth. Multilingual students, by bringing their language to the classrooms, weave a diverse linguistic tapestry to schools, enriching the learning experience for all.

6 Unlocking the diversity of EAL students

Multilingual Learner Profile			
Name	Year	English Language Proficiency	Language(s)
Adam (M) TEKLE	7	B (Early Acquisition)	Tigrinya English

Language	Speaking	Listening	Reading	Writing
Tigrinya	✓	✓	✓	✓
English	B	B	B	B

Adam was born in Eritrea and lived there until the age of 9. He attended primary school in Eritrea and is literate in Tigrinya. He left Eritrea at the age of 9 and lived in Ethiopia for several months, during which he did not attend school. The family, which includes Adam's mother and older sister, moved to the Netherlands for a few weeks, where Adam began learning Dutch. Additionally, Adam has also learned some Amharic and Arabic.

Adam can use a computer but might require some support. He enjoys drawing and painting and is interested in joining sports clubs.

Adam's English language proficiency level is B (Early Acquisition) and will need a considerable level of support to access mainstream lessons.

Figure 1.1 Profiles of multilingual learners can be shared with teaching and support staff prior to the students' first day in mainstream lessons. These profiles offer concise information about the students' backgrounds, enabling the creation of a supportive and inclusive environment, as well as effective support.

As a staff member introduces Adam to you, you remember that he originally comes from Eritrea, where he was born and lived with his family until the age of nine, attending school there. Adam is literate in Tigrinya, which he uses to communicate with his family, including his mother and an older sister. The family decided to leave their home country due to the unstable political situation. Over several months, they journeyed to the United Kingdom, briefly staying in Ethiopia and the Netherlands along the way. During their time in Ethiopia, Adam did not have access to formal schooling but managed to make many friends who spoke languages like Amharic, Arabic and English, among others. Upon arriving in the Netherlands, Adam began to learn Dutch and received some intensive survival language lessons. Ultimately, Adam's family moved to England to reunite with friends and distant relatives who had embarked on a similar journey several years prior. These friends and relatives provided invaluable assistance to Adam's mother by helping her with essential paperwork and guiding her through the process of applying for a secondary school placement for Adam.

Who are EAL learners?

Adam's journey, while marked by turbulence and considerable length, is not unusual. Multilingual students and their families may come to the UK for various reasons, and their legal status can vary depending on their specific circumstances.

Some common reasons for multilingual students and their families to come to the UK include:

- **asylum seekers and refugees:** some students and their families arrive in the UK as asylum seekers or refugees, fleeing persecution, conflict or humanitarian crises in their home countries.
- **economic opportunities:** others may come to the UK in search of better economic opportunities and work offers. Skilled workers and professionals may come to the UK for job opportunities, and their legal status would be linked to their work visas or permits.
- education: some multilingual students' families come to the UK for educational opportunities, often to pursue higher education or language courses.
- **family reunification**: family members of individuals already residing in the UK may come to reunite with their loved ones.
- **marriage or partnership:** multilingual students and their families may arrive in the UK due to marriage or partnership with a British citizen or someone with legal residence status.

It is important to note that the legal status of EAL students and their families can vary greatly based on their specific circumstances and the type of visas or permits they hold. Some may have moved to the UK permanently, while others may have a defined length of stay and some may not have concrete plans, relying on immigration services' decisions. Many students are first-, second- or third-generation children born in the UK and may have never left the country. It is evident that multilingual children in our schools have diverse educational experiences, use various languages at different proficiency levels and possess varying legal and socioeconomic statuses. All these factors contribute to their unique life experiences in multiple ways.

As previously mentioned, Adam will be among the 20% of multilingual learners in nurseries, primary and secondary state-funded schools in England. However, the composition of multilingual learners in his school can vary widely. In some schools, multilingual learners may represent only a small minority, comprising just a few students. In other cases, they may make up the majority, accounting for 70% or even 80% of the school's population. It is important to note that these figures may not always be accurate. Many schools do not consistently apply the definition of EAL to their learners, particularly if they were born in England or have highly developed English language proficiency. Failure to record students' heritage languages can unintentionally devalue these languages and suggest a lack of appreciation for students' cultural heritages.

Similarly, if we only recognise students as EAL learners when their English language proficiency indicates they are newcomers or at the early stages of language acquisition, we risk adopting a deficit-based perspective, primarily focusing on English. While proficiency in English is essential, given its role as the language of instruction and examination in English schools, it is crucial to avoid creating a hierarchical approach to languages. A particular language or dialect may be spoken by only a handful of students in a school with hundreds or thousands of learners, but it remains a vital language within the child's family and home environment.

We should ensure that **all languages are valued**. This can be emphasised during new student admissions meetings or parents' meetings and evenings. It could also be integrated into the school's language and broader policies to ensure that all families, staff members and visitors are aware of the school's stance on this matter. Making parents aware of the number of multilingual students and staff, as well as the languages spoken by them, may encourage families to share their linguistic backgrounds and heritages. Regrettably, for various reasons, many families may be reluctant to disclose or share information about the languages used within their households. I recall being in an admissions meeting where a mother adamantly advised a staff member not to classify her daughter as an EAL student, despite having just spoken to her daughter in a different language moments earlier, and receiving a response in her first language. It is important to respect families' choices, as some discussions may involve sensitive matters. However, it is crucial to inform them about the school's **commitment to linguistic inclusiveness** from the outset.

In many conversations with families, it has become evident that many of them recognise the significant advantages and even the obligation to maintain and develop their first languages. First and foremost, they highlight that the language they speak is an integral part of their identity. Secondly, they use it to communicate with family and friends, whether in the UK or in their home countries. At Trinity Academy Leeds, we have observed that our students are eager to share their linguistic heritages and engage in discussions with teachers and peers. They take pride in their multilingualism and are encouraged to further develop their language skills and pursue GCSE Heritage Language exams. Their linguistic knowledge enhances the learning experience for all students in our lessons. For example, students who speak Greek provide valuable insights into words with Greek origins, Urdu-speaking learners contribute significantly when we study works like *I am Malala* by Malala Yousafzai and our Nigerian students offer a deeper and more detailed understanding of the culture and characters depicted by Chimamanda Ngozi Adichie in *Purple Hibiscus*.

> You warmly greet Adam and ask him to take a seat next to Ana, who speaks Romanian. Ana has been living in England since she was five years old and is an advanced bilingual student. Adam is joining your class toward the end of the term and you have some concerns that he may not fully understand the lesson or actively participate. You also realise that Adam is likely feeling a bit nervous, but you notice a faint smile on his face when Ana gives him a quick wave and says, 'Hi!'. Starting a new secondary school can be a stressful experience for any 11-year-old. Adam will face the same potentially stress-inducing challenges that come with adjusting to a new environment, such as making new friends, forming social circles, finding his way around a large school building, learning the names of teachers, keeping up with homework assignments and remembering to bring his PE kit twice

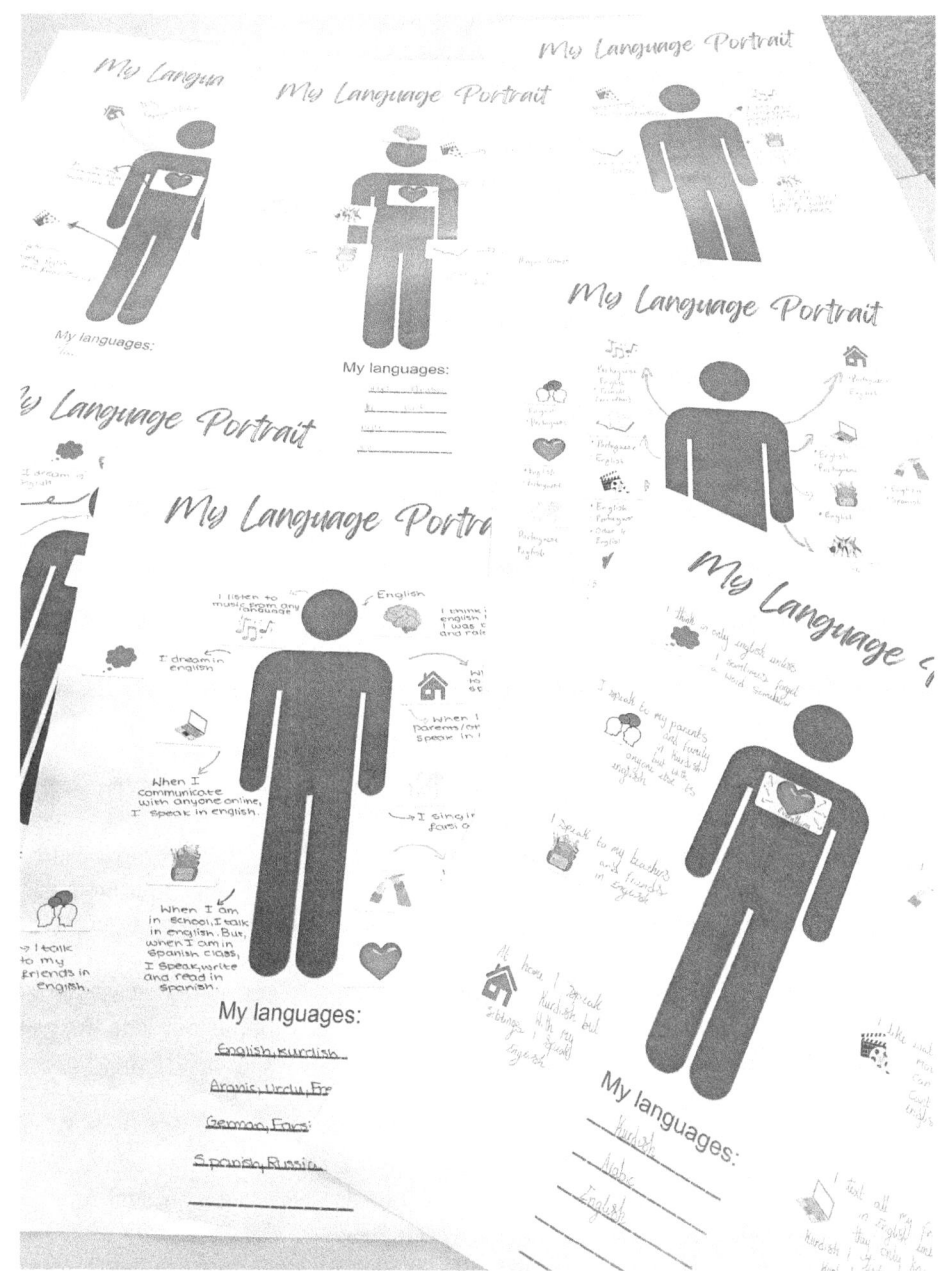

Figure 1.2 At Trinity Academy Leeds, students take pride in their multilingualism. They understand the power and significance of different languages in their lives.

a week. Additionally, he will need to absorb a considerable amount of new information across various subjects. Adam will undergo ongoing, informal assessments in day-to-day activities, as well as formal end-of-term and end-of-year assessments. All of this in a language that is new to him.

Who and how teaches EAL learners?

Whether you are an Early Career Teacher (ECT), an educator with several years of teaching experience or a highly experienced professional with decades in the classroom, the responsibility of teaching English as an additional language learners is shared among all teachers in your school. The Teachers' Standards, as outlined by the Department for Education, do briefly reference EAL pupils within Standard 5. It emphasises that teachers should have a clear understanding of the **needs of all students**, including those with EAL, and be **capable of using appropriate approaches** to support them on their academic journey (Department of Education, 2021). How confident are you in your ability to possess the requisite skills and expertise to effectively support multilingual learners in your classroom? Does your school or a broader educational network provide any training opportunities to enhance your pedagogical approaches for working with EAL learners? Is there a shared understanding within your school of what constitutes high-yielding and effective support for EAL students at various English language proficiency levels? Considering students like Adam joining your class, how do you feel? What proactive steps will you take to ensure that he thrives academically in your subject?

A research report published in 2018 strongly recommends shifting the mindset regarding English as an Additional Language from being a specialised area to an integral aspect of teacher education. Our goal should be to encourage and support teachers in making all lessons more accessible to multilingual and multicultural classes, treating **multilingualism and multiculturalism as the new norm in mainstream education** (Foley et al., 2018). The report also suggests implementing a 'dual' approach to EAL development within teacher education programmes. This approach involves providing foundational knowledge and strategies, followed by the integration of EAL considerations throughout individual subjects and core teacher education, ensuring that EAL is a central and subject-specific focus.

The experiences of multilingual students, such as Adam, can vary significantly in English schools. His experiences will depend strongly on the understanding of the school, teachers and every member of the staff that all multilingual learners have the right to access an ambitious and age-appropriate curriculum. They also have the right to full support in accessing this curriculum, which encompasses both **content and language development**. Teaching EAL students involves a comprehensive approach to language learning that considers functional, social and academic skills within an English-speaking environment. In many aspects, it differs from other approaches, and it is crucial to understand these differences while also recognising the overlaps to ensure that EAL students receive the same high-quality secondary education as other learners.

The teaching and learning of the English language is a dynamic and evolving field that adapts to the changing goals of learners. It encompasses a wide range of approaches, influenced by factors such as geographical location, learning objectives, student characteristics and instructional methodologies. Various terminologies have been developed to capture these diverse aspects. While there are certain similarities and overlaps among different programmes, they also possess distinct features. It is crucial to avoid conflating them, as doing so might inadvertently place learners at a disadvantage.

The term **English Language Teaching** (ELT) is commonly employed to denote an educational field dedicated to teaching English as a second or foreign language. It is an umbrella term for ELT programmes and courses which can be found in schools, language institutes, universities and online platforms worldwide. Their main aim is to develop learners' communicative competence, enabling them to effectively use English for a myriad of purposes, ranging from personal enrichment, professional communication, travel to academic study regardless of whether English is the main language.

English as Foreign Language (EFL) pertains to learning of English in a country where English is not the primary language and is distinct from the first language of the learners. This category encompasses educational institutions, both public and private, where English is taught as a subject to school-age children, teenagers preparing for language examinations and adults seeking proficiency for work, travel or other personal reasons.

English as a Second Language (ESL) refers to teaching English to learners in countries where English is the dominant language but not their first language. ESL learners could be immigrants, international students or individuals living in English-speaking communities who need English language skills for everyday communication, education or work. ESOL (English for Speakers of Other Languages) is another inclusive term that covers the teaching of English speakers of languages other than English. Often it is used in the context of post- secondary or adult education as well as community-based language programmes.

English for Academic Purposes (EAP) focuses on teaching English language skills which are essential for academic context. They are designed with students who use a language other than English in mind, particularly those who intend to pursue higher education or engage in academic study in an English-speaking environment. Pre-sessional university programmes, which are quite popular in the United Kingdom, typically prioritise academic reading and writing as well as research and presentation skills. EAP programmes aim to cultivate students' general academic skills whereas English for Specific Purposes (ESP) entails the teaching of English tailored to particular academic, professional or vocational contexts. This specialised approach concentrates on the development of language skills and knowledge pertinent to specific fields of study such as English for Medicine, English for Business or English for Engineering.

Content and Language Integrated Learning (CLIL) is an educational approach that aims to teach both content knowledge and language skills simultaneously. It involves delivering academic subjects, such as science, history or mathematics, through a target language. CLIL programmes integrate language learning with subject-specific content and allow students to develop language proficiency while acquiring knowledge in various disciplines. The actual number of CLIL lessons will vary depending on my factors, such as the school's curriculum or resources of the school just to name a couple. In some schools, CLIL may be implemented as a specific subject or course, where a substantial proportion of the curriculum is taught in the target language. CLIL is often implemented in bilingual or multilingual educational settings, where students have a strong foundation in their first language and are learning another one, such as English, as a medium of instruction.

Similarly to CLIL, **Bilingual Education** (BE) involves the instruction and use of two languages. In BE, however, the two languages serve as mediums of instruction. The aim is to develop students' proficiency and academic skills in both languages, typically their first or heritage language and a second language, which typically is the main language of the region or country. There are different models and approaches to bilingual education but they all strive to develop students as bilingual and biliterate users of two languages.

The teaching of English as an Additional Language (EAL) has many crossovers and similarities with the CLIL approach as it should, in theory, aim to develop both content and language simultaneously. The main difference is that EAL students whose first language is different from English, attend mainstream classes where the language of instruction is English for every single lesson. Some EAL learners, depending on their English language

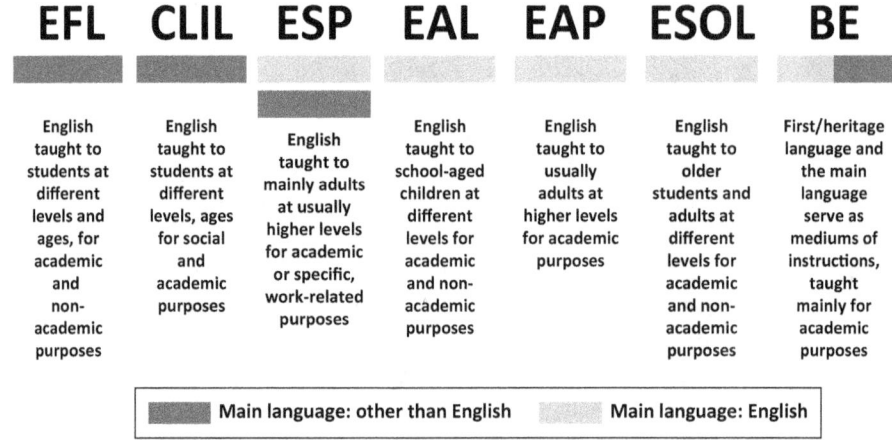

Figure 1.3 English Language Teaching encompasses many different contexts in which the English language is taught. There are some overlaps and distinctive features between these approaches.

proficiency levels, prior education and attainment, might require ongoing or very personalised language support in order to access lessons. In addition to fostering English language proficiency for academic purposes, EAL learners rely on English to communicate in various everyday contexts in and outside of school.

> As a starter activity, the class is answering questions about the Nile Delta. You hand a piece of paper to Adam with the initial task he needs to complete. It is a map of Africa with arrows pointing to the Nile River, Egypt, Sudan and the Sahara Desert. You point at the pen and say, 'Write in Tigrinya'. Adam nods and starts writing right away. It takes him less than a minute to label the map. You identify and highlight the key words and expressions from the starter questions on the whiteboard and ask Adam to write the English equivalents next to the words in Tigrinya. When Adam correctly completes the first word, he receives a 'thumbs up' from Ana. Adam is feeling a bit less worried now. It seems that his new class is studying something he learned over three years ago.

It is undeniable that joining a new school and learning new things in a new language can be extremely challenging. Teachers may also find teaching multilingual learners, particularly those who are new to English or have experienced interrupted formal education, to be quite demanding and, in many cases, daunting. Let's remind ourselves that the terms EAL or multilingual indicate that students are learning English as an additional language while already being able to communicate in at least one, if not multiple, languages.

The Common Underlying Proficiency (CUP) serves as a theoretical framework that explains how bilingual and multilingual individuals utilise their language abilities across different languages (Cummins, 1979). CUP posits that all languages known by a multilingual student share a common underlying proficiency or a set of cognitive and linguistic skills. These skills are not specific to any single language but form a cognitive foundation upon which multiple languages can be built. CUP also suggests that if a person can use one language, they can use their cognitive and linguistic skills to facilitate learning and proficiency in a second language. The languages that a student knows are interconnected and this interconnectedness can positively impact the development of all language skills. In educational contexts, this interconnectedness can be especially beneficial, as students may use their existing language skills to aid the acquisition of a new language and new information.

Importantly, these languages were not learned in isolation. All multilingual learners bring their 'funds of knowledge' to our classrooms, and their diverse backgrounds and experiences represent valuable assets for their education (Gonzalez, 2005). It is imperative that we recognise and leverage the cultural and linguistic resources of our students while they are developing proficiency in a new language. The key questions are: what are the prerequisites for a child to acquire a language? How long does this process take? Is learning a second language akin to or distinct from learning or acquiring the first language? Understanding both first and second language acquisition is indispensable for educators

Theories about first language acquisition

Learning a language is an extremely nuanced process and current theories combine different elements introduced and presented by many prominent researchers. Rather than perceiving theoretical perspectives as residing on two ends of the extreme, it is sensible to imagine them on a cline as each theory comes with its own strengths and weaknesses.

One of the most influential approaches has been innatism proposed by Noam Chomsky, which suggests that humans have an innate ability to learn language and this capacity is biologically determined. **The theory of innatism** suggests that the innate ability to learn language is specific only to humans. Chomsky argues that the process of language acquisition is driven by a **universal grammar**, a set of innate principles that underlies all human languages and guides the child's ability to learn the specific grammar of a language. According to this theory, children are born with a '**language acquisition device**' that allows them to extract the underlying grammatical structure of a language, regardless of the specific language they are exposed to. Chomsky also points out that children are able to learn language at an astonishingly fast rate with minimal input, which is seen as evidence of the existence of an innate language ability.

If we were to employ a dichotomous view on learning a language, **the theory of behaviourism** would be proposed in opposition to innatism. Behaviourism is a theory associated with B. F. Skinner and argues that language acquisition is a result of operant conditioning, where children learn language through **reinforcement and imitation**. They are reinforced for producing language that is similar to the language they hear from others, and they imitate the language they hear in their environment. The theory emphasises the role of the environment and the interactions between the child and their caregivers in shaping language acquisition. B. F. Skinner argued that children learn language through a process of trial and error. They try out different sounds and words and are reinforced for the ones that are similar to the language they hear around them. The theory also claims that children's language develops through a process of shaping, where small approximations to adult speech are gradually reinforced and strengthened. The behaviourist theory was a dominant perspective in the field of psychology and education during the 1950s and 1960s, but it has since been criticised for not being able to account for the complex structure of language and the child's ability to generate new language forms.

Subsequently, **the theory of interactionism** was proposed as a middle ground between innatism and behaviourism as it recognises the importance of both **innate abilities and environmental factors** in language acquisition. Interactionism resides on the latter side of the Nature vs Nurture opposition. This theory in language acquisition was popularised by several scholars in the field of sociolinguistics, education and sociocultural theory, but one of the most prominent key figures associated with this approach is a Russian psychologist and philosopher, Lev Vygotsky. He proposed that **language is a social and cultural phenomenon** shaped by the social interactions of the learner. Children learn language through meaningful social interactions with others, and that language development is influenced by social, cultural and environmental factors. Language learning is seen as **a collaborative process** and active participation and interaction between the learner and their environment is required. Whilst a child is interacting with others, they actively use language and receive feedback which allows them to gradually develop an understanding of how language works (Ellis, 2000; Lightbown and Spada, 2003).

The importance of recognising various contexts in which language is used is crucial to language learning according to this theory. The social and cultural contexts shape language learning. Children quickly learn and recognise various social norms and language conventions which are attached to a variety of situations. They adjust the language depending on the situation they are in, and will probably switch from using a more casual language with friends to a more formal form of language in a classroom and school setting. Importantly, the theory of social interactionist theory suggests that language learning is heavily influenced by the quantity and quality of social interactions which a child participates in and is exposed to. If children have plenty of opportunities to engage in meaningful conversations with speakers of the same language, either adults or peers, they are more likely to develop stronger foundations to enhance their language skills. Those who do not experience high-quality and regular exchanges, seem to be at a disadvantage as they do not have access to scaffolding, or support, for their language development. This support, which can take many forms of modelling language, providing feedback, offering guidance and support, is a critical factor in the development of higher-order cognitive functions. Language is not purely a form of communication, but as it closely links to broader cultural and social practices, it is a tool through which our thinking and problem-solving skills are materialised.

Similarly, other language learning theories emphasise the active role of the learner in constructing linguistic knowledge. **The connectionist theory** is a cognitive approach to language development which proposes that language learning is based on neural networks and connections in the brain. The interconnected web of neurons is reinforced every time a child encounters a given word in a particular context. When the same word is used in a different scenario with potentially other meanings but the same pronunciation, a new connection is formed and the highly intertwined system expands. Language learning is perceived as the process of forming and strengthening connections between various language-related elements in the brain, such as sounds, words and meanings. **The active construction of grammar theory** also highlights the active role of the learners in the language acquisition process. Children are thought to **actively construct their own grammar rules** based on the input they receive, mainly on the language they hear around them. The language acquisition process, therefore, is ongoing and involves cognitive processes: children test, trial, revise and adjust their grammar rules based on the input they receive. The input is an active source of information, and children are able to adapt their language to suit the linguistic environment they are in. Language that we learn is not constant and set in stone – it is flexible, dynamic and constantly evolving (Ellis, 2000)

Another theory which emphasises the importance of usage and experience in shaping linguistic knowledge rather than relying purely on innate or explicit knowledge of rules governing a language is **the usage-based theory**. Analogously to the active grammar construction theory, the usage-based theory claims that learners gradually **build a mental representation of language** because they interact with it in a meaningful and frequent manner. In the latter approach, however, **the learners are seen as pattern-seekers**. They notice regularities in language and observe associations and connections between the elements of language instead of inventing and reinventing the rules based on the known and newly received input.

Theories about second language acquisition

Second language acquisition theories offer some unique perspectives on how individuals acquire a second language, reflecting diverse approaches, cognitive processes and external influences. While these theories have been developed primarily to explain the acquisition of second languages, they also intersect with the study of first language acquisition and offer insight into language development across the lifespan, which is something that is applicable to all multilingual learners.

Behaviourist theory, a prominent concept in the field of psychology and education which has been discussed earlier, has also been applied to the study of second language acquisition. In the context of second language acquisition, behaviourist theory suggests that language learning is **a product of external factors**, such as reinforcement, repetition and imitation of language patterns and structures. It draws on the idea that language learning is **a habit-forming process**, where learners respond to stimuli, such as correct language usage or reinforcement from teachers and peers. In practice, this theory led to methodologies like audiolingualism, where language learners were exposed to a great deal of repetition and drilling of language patterns. Behaviourist principles were thought to be particularly effective for teaching basic language skills and promoting accuracy in language production. Contemporary research on second language acquisition, however, has moved beyond strict behaviourism. It has been recognised that learning a new language is a much more complex process, influenced by factors such as cognitive development or social interaction. The behaviourist principles can still be useful in language instruction for EAL learners. For example, introducing sentence starters and building in opportunities for students to use them on multiple occasions and memorise them, will result in students recalling sentence stems with ease. Of course, these drills and repetitions must be used judiciously and integrated into more comprehensive tasks which takes into account creative and spontaneous language use.

In the context of second language acquisition, the **innatist theory** suggests that the same universal principles that underlie first language acquisition also play a role in the acquisition of additional languages. Learners are believed to tap into their **innate language abilities** when learning a new language. This theory stands in contrast to behaviourist theories which emphasise external stimuli whilst the innatist theory suggests that humans have **an inherent capacity for language** and this makes language acquisition more than just a set of learnt behaviours. While this theory focuses on the biological basis of language acquisition, it does not negate the significance of social environment factors. In fact, social interaction as emphasised by Vygotsky is seen as the means through which innate language abilities are activated and developed (Ellis, 2000; Lightbown and Spada, 2003; Saville-Troike, 2006).

This theory has led to the hypothesis that there may be a '**critical period**' or 'sensitive period' for language acquisition, during which the innate language abilities are most effective and language acquisition is most effective. It suggests that there is a biologically determined window of time during which language acquisition is most effective. There may be an advantage to learning a second language at a younger age in terms of pronunciation and fluency. While there is some consensus that age plays a significant role in second language learning, it is just one of several factors to be considered when supporting multilingual learners. As educators, our primary focus should be on the quality and quantity of language that students are exposed to and engage with, and how these factors inform our approach to planning for multilingual students (Sharples, 2021).

The **input theory**, which belongs to cognitive theories and has been championed by Stephen Krashen, is one of the most influential in the field of second language acquisition. It explains how learners acquire a second language through **comprehensible input** (Krashen, 1982, 1985). It suggests that language learners acquire language most effectively when they are exposed to input which is just slightly beyond their current level of linguistic competence. In other words, learners need exposure to language that is challenging but not so complex that it overwhelms them. Krashen's theory aligns with the idea that language acquisition occurs in a manner similar to how individuals naturally acquire their first languages. While it is easy to concur with the points made above, implementing them in mainstream lessons can prove to be considerably more challenging. First and foremost, it is improbable that a child's first language was acquired during periods when they were expected to grasp and proficiently respond to cognitively demanding tasks, such as answering science or English literature exam questions. Secondly, when a new student who is new to English joins your class, it is expected that there will be portions of the lessons that, from a linguistic perspective, are simply too intricate and demanding for them, which can indeed be overwhelming. Krashen suggests that teachers should prioritise **meaningful language input** rather than placing excessive emphasis on grammar drills or explicit instruction. While it is essential to 'immerse' students in subject classrooms, enabling them to actively participate in mainstream lessons, it is equally vital to ensure the presence of a well-thought-out language support component that complements the content planning.

The complexity and diversity of factors involved in language acquisition, coupled with ethical considerations and logistical challenges, contribute to our incomplete understanding of how languages are learned. While researchers have made significant progress and continue to explore this field, language acquisition remains a multifaceted and evolving area of study. Comparing first and second language acquisition theories provides a unique perspective for examining the commonalities and differences between these two fundamental aspects of human language development. Within the context of education and working with EAL learners in mainstream classrooms, second language acquisition theories offer invaluable insights into the practical applications of these theories in the classroom. This includes curriculum design and instructional strategies that facilitate the linguistic and academic development of multilingual learners. These theories also emphasise the distinctive nature of effective teaching and learning for multilingual learners in their day-to-day experiences.

> You transition to the main part of the lesson, where the class will delve into the River Nile's significance in transportation and its role in the development of ancient civilisations. You will also explore its importance in modern times. Throughout the lesson, you utilise visuals to illustrate the array of resources transported on the river and the types of boats used in both ancient and contemporary contexts. As the entire class listens, you employ a visualiser to point to the images that complement the text's description. You rephrase certain sentences and pose comprehension questions to ensure that students grasp the ideas conveyed in the text. For Adam's benefit, you provide a word mat containing key vocabulary and sentence starters. When students are tasked with discussing questions in pairs, he endeavours to complete sentences like: 'In ancient times, people transported _____. Now, people transport _____'. He also uses this resource independently to compose a brief response to the question: 'Why is the River Nile important for transportation?'

What is good practice for EAL learners?

How successful and effective was this lesson for Adam? Arguably, there are various factors we could use to assess the lesson's effectiveness, even if focusing on this specific student. One might assert, and it would be hard to dispute, that by the end of the lesson, Adam may not be able to confidently articulate the significance of the River Nile concerning the development of the transportation system, especially if asked to use detailed and well-developed sentences in English. He might not be capable of confidently reading a paragraph or composing a cohesive answer in English. However, it is crucial not to undervalue Adam's accomplishments in this geography lesson. What Adam achieved was a small but important step in his education in a new country. Language acquisition and learning through English is not something that can be accomplished in a relatively short time frame; it is indeed **a lengthy process**. We might not always discern the incremental changes and developments in a student's language acquisition on a daily basis. Yet, many teachers have noted remarkable progress in multilingual learners over the span of a few months, a term or an academic year.

Considering the principles of second language acquisition theories, which emphasise students' exposure to language, the social aspect of language learning and the ability to practise new linguistic forms, **mainstream lessons provide the ideal environment** to offer these opportunities. Furthermore, mainstream classes are where students are exposed to content and language simultaneously, practise using the language with their peers within the curriculum and have the chance to rehearse new language pertaining to all subject areas. These factors, coupled with scaffolding language, promoting cultural awareness, fostering inclusion and providing supportive feedback, contribute to the best practices for multilingual learners (Gibbons, 1993, 2015).

While some learners may benefit from a tailored support program, whether on a one-to-one basis or in small groups, delivered over several weeks alongside attending mainstream classes, others may integrate directly into mainstream classes. For some, it could be beneficial if intense, language and content-driven sessions were provided. There is no one-size-fits-all formula; the support should be flexible and proactive, tailored to serve the students in the most advantageous manner. Gaining insights into EAL students, their previous educational history, family circumstances, spoken languages, literacy levels in those languages and the duration of time spent in other countries and in England will enable us to ensure that students receive the most effective support.

> It is March, and it has been five months since Adam attended his first geography lesson. During this time, he has made some friends, joined an after-school art club and has been encouraged by his PE teacher to participate in rugby training sessions. He can confidently communicate with other students and during breaks and lunchtime, he is always surrounded by a group of Year 7 students, laughing or discussing their plans for the weekend. In geography and other lessons, he works with high levels of motivation, completes his homework on time, articulates his answers effectively and is always eager to ask questions when he encounters something he does not understand. Additionally, he participates in a small group of multilingual Year 7 students twice a week, where he receives support to further enhance his reading and writing skills. The sessions, delivered by a specialist EAL teacher, are co-planned with subject teachers and revolve around the topics studied in mainstream lessons. However, the most recent independent piece of writing has revealed that while Adam comprehends most of the concepts studied in lessons, his written responses lack coherence, feature inaccurately structured sentences and often confuse the reader due to issues with prepositions and tenses. His use of pronouns is also inconsistent and he needs to practise spelling of some subject-specific as well as high-frequency words. It is evident that Adam's language development requires support from you and every teacher throughout this year and all the way through to Year 11, as the cognitive demands of the curriculum, as well as the complexity of the language, increase year by year.

How long does it take to learn a new language?

In 2017, English language proficiency levels of all EAL students in English schools were assessed using a five-point scale. Before this, schools may or may not have evaluated the English language proficiency levels of multilingual students, and if they did, they might

20 *Unlocking the diversity of EAL students*

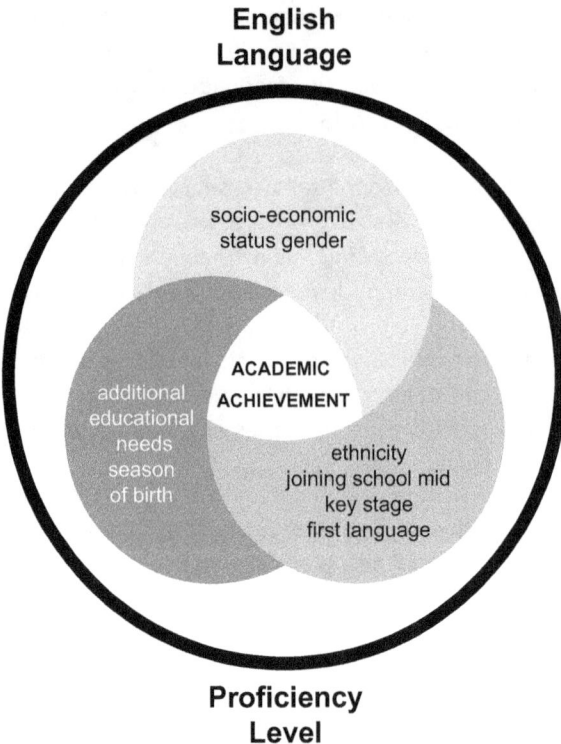

Figure 1.4 English language proficiency levels are the strongest indicators of a multilingual learner's academic attainment.

have employed various scales and frameworks. The 2017 census not only documented the linguistic diversity in English schools but also emphasised the correlation between **English proficiency levels** and students' overall academic achievement. Subsequent research, which analysed national and local data, concluded that although many factors contribute to students' academic success, proficiency in the English language is the most influential (Strand and Hessel, 2018; Strand and Lindorff, 2020).

The levels and their descriptors

A (New to English): these individuals may predominantly rely on their first language for learning and other purposes. They might choose to remain silent in class, mimic or repeat words and phrases and grasp basic everyday English expressions. Their English language proficiency levels necessitate extensive support in mainstream classrooms.

B (Early Acquisition): learners at this stage can comprehend daily social communication in English with some assistance. They are starting to use spoken English for social interactions, understand simple instructions and follow narratives with visual aids. They may possess basic reading and writing skills and some subject-specific vocabulary. Nevertheless, they still require substantial EAL support to access the curriculum.

- **C (Developing Competence):** these students can engage in learning activities with increasing self-reliance. They can express themselves verbally in English, although some structural errors may be evident. Literacy skills, particularly in reading and writing, need ongoing assistance. They can handle more abstract concepts and intricate written English, but they still rely on EAL support to fully access the curriculum.
- **D (Competent):** individuals at this stage have well-developed spoken English skills, enabling them to effectively participate in various curriculum tasks. They can read and understand a wide array of texts. Their written English may lack complexity and may occasionally contain structural mistakes. They need some help to grasp subtle meanings, improve English usage and expand their abstract vocabulary. Occasional EAL support is required to access complex curriculum materials and assignments.
- **E (Fluent):** at this level, students can function across the curriculum with a level of competence comparable to that of native speakers. While a complete description of this level is not provided, it suggests a high level of English proficiency and independence in using the language.

In this book, I will refer to the descriptors as outlined above. The Bell Foundation, a UK-based charity organisation that focuses on promoting educational and language development for individuals learning English as an additional language, has developed a comprehensive framework for assessing EAL learners and provides detailed descriptions for each skill: speaking, listening, reading and writing at each level. The descriptors are available online at www.bell-foundation.org.uk.

Just as learning a new language is a lengthy process, it is equally complex. Students' **language development is not linear** and often uneven in terms of developing different skills. Adam's spoken, everyday conversational English would likely be described at a C level, as he can communicate easily with his friends and staff members. During lessons, he can provide detailed answers, albeit with occasional grammar or vocabulary inaccuracies, which become even more evident in his writing. Although he can decode and read words with confidence, there are some words and expressions that he is unfamiliar with, often affecting his comprehension of substantial portions of texts. Adam's written responses might be described as B.

It is not possible to definitively state how long it takes for an individual to learn a new language and use it proficiently across all skills. **Language learning is a complex and individualised process** influenced by various factors, as mentioned before: age, the learner's prior linguistic and educational background, the intensity of language exposure and the context in which the language is acquired. One of the most influential concepts widely used in the fields of bilingual education and second language learning is the notion of **Basic Interpersonal Communicative Skills** (BICS) and **Cognitive Academic Language Proficiency** (CALP), introduced by Professor Jim Cummins. He formulated these concepts based on his research and observations of students who were learning English (Cummins, 1984). While their spoken everyday skills developed rapidly, many of their teachers expressed concerns about these students not following a similar trajectory, particularly when engaging with more complex, conceptually advanced written materials.

According to Cummins, BICS represent the ability to engage in conversations, interact with friends and family and participate in casual social situations.

The characteristics of BICS include:

- **everyday communication skills:** BICS encompass the language skills needed for common, day-to-day interactions. This includes speaking and understanding language in familiar contexts, such as talking to friends, family members, classmates or colleagues.
- **conversational fluency:** BICS reflect conversational fluency, allowing individuals to engage in small talk and routine conversations. People with strong BICS can comfortably discuss everyday topics, express their feelings and understand the gist of what others are saying.
- **context-embedded:** BICS are context-embedded, which means they heavily rely on the immediate context, non-verbal cues and situational factors. In casual conversations, people often use body language, tone of voice and shared knowledge to aid comprehension.
- **quick development:** language learners typically acquire BICS relatively quickly, often within a year or two of immersion in the environment where a language is used. This might be because everyday communication is generally more straightforward than the language's structural and academic aspects.

CALP is a crucial concept in language education, as it highlights the distinction between basic social language skills (BICS) and the more complex academic language skills necessary for educational achievement.

The characteristics of CALP include:

- **academic skills:** CALP encompasses the language skills necessary for academic success. It involves the ability to comprehend and use language at a higher level, particularly when engaging with complex subject matter and intellectual tasks.
- **context-reduced:** CALP is context-reduced, meaning it relies less on immediate context and more on a deep understanding of the language's structural and academic components. It is used in situations where the context alone might not provide sufficient clues for comprehension.
- **advanced language proficiency:** CALP proficiency goes beyond everyday conversational language. It includes the ability to read, write and discuss academic topics, as well as to engage in analytical reasoning using the language.
- **longer development time:** developing CALP proficiency typically takes a longer time and often necessitates explicit instruction, practice and exposure to academic language. This is because it involves a more intricate understanding of the language's grammar, vocabulary and specialised terminology.

Cummins estimated that, on average, it takes a student who is new to English **five to seven years to develop CALP**. Most recently, these claims have been confirmed by several

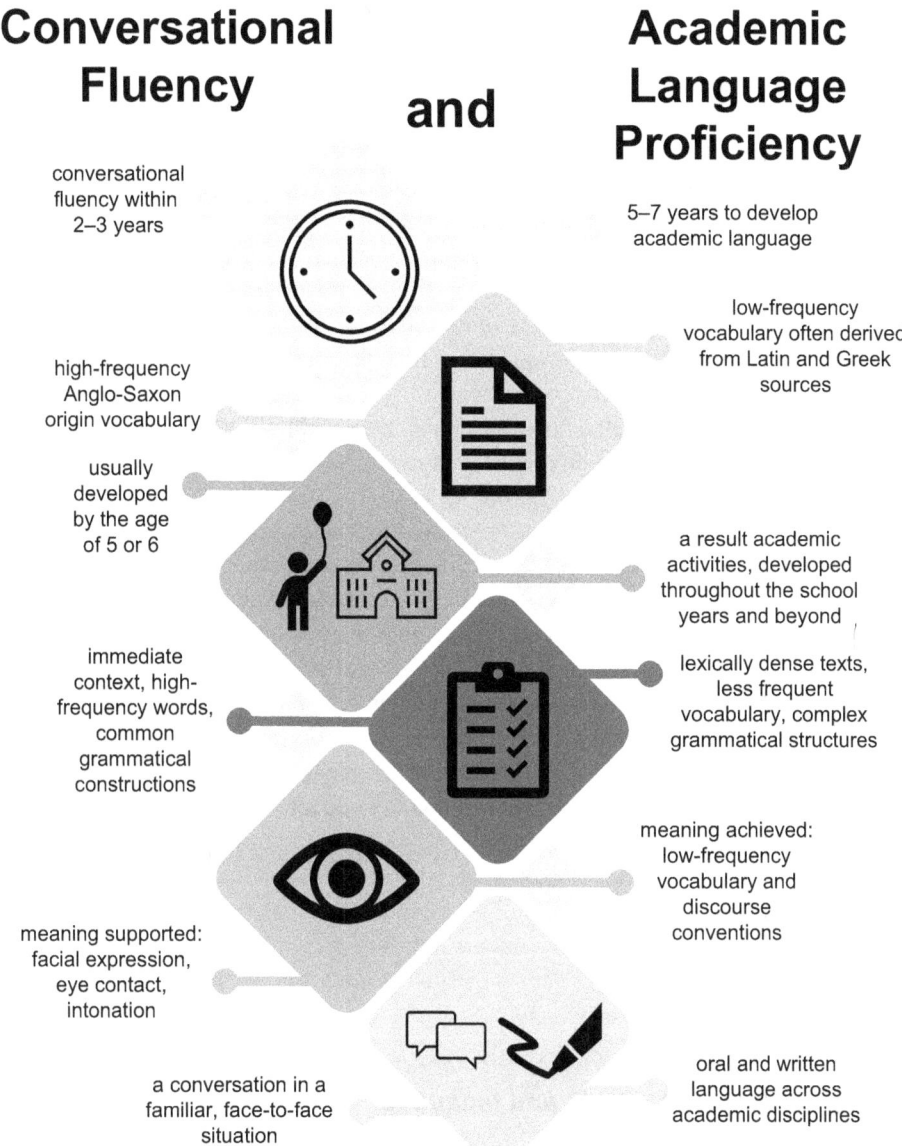

Figure 1.5 Conversational and academic language proficiency are both important to multilingual learners' language development. Adapted from: Cummins, J. 2021. **Rethinking the Education of Multilingual Learners.** Bristol: Multilingual Matters.

researchers who conducted longitudinal studies in the UK, encompassing students at various initial stages and rates of progression (Demie, 2013; Strand and Lindorff, 2020). The findings underscore the significance of supporting students' language development long after they appear to have reached a level where they comprehend lessons and can participate in classroom activities. Teachers and the school system play a vital role in helping EAL learners develop both BICS and CALP. Recognising the importance of these two language domains allows for more targeted and effective language instruction and support, ultimately enhancing the overall educational and life outcomes of multilingual learners.

While widely influential and valuable in understanding language acquisition and language education, the BICS and CALP framework have also encountered criticism and debate. Some critics argue that the BICS and CALP framework oversimplifies the complex nature of language proficiency, contending that language proficiency is a multidimensional phenomenon that cannot be neatly divided into just two categories. Additionally, some argue that the framework may inadvertently reinforce an artificial division between academic and social language. In reality, academic language often includes social and conversational elements, and these distinctions are not always clear-cut. Lastly, it has been pointed out that the BICS and CALP division could have sociopolitical implications. For example, the framework might be used to label certain groups of students as 'deficient' in one or both areas of language proficiency, potentially perpetuating biases and inequalities in education.

Cummins continues to refine and expand upon his ideas in response to criticism and has addressed and acknowledged this in one of his recent publications (Cummins, 2021). He agrees that **language proficiency is multifaceted** but argues that the BICS and CALP distinction helps education and researchers focus on the differing language demands in social and academic contexts. Cummins has also been concerned about the potential misuse of his framework to label and stigmatise students. He has stressed that language proficiency levels should not be used to disadvantage and discriminate against any group. Cummins has advocated for **inclusive and equitable language education policies for all students**, regardless of whether they are monolingual or multilingual. Lastly, he clarified that the BICS and CALP framework does not rigidly separate academic and social language. He acknowledges they overlap and that students need both types of language for their academic and social success. These two areas are not seen as dichotomous but complementing one another. Just as all languages should be seen as important, all types of language need to be recognised as valuable too.

The perfect match: content and language

At the centre of this book is the belief that all learners, including multilingual learners who are at different stages of acquiring the English language, should have access to **an ambitious, level-appropriate curriculum** that not only challenges and inspires them but also aligns with their language proficiency. Teaching and learning of the **language** should not run in parallel to the subject matter but it should be intertwined, **inseparable and taught simultaneously**.

Language and content are deeply intertwined and teaching them simultaneously is essential for multilingual learners in mainstream classrooms. Language is the key to accessing and understanding academic content. When EAL learners are introduced to subject matter

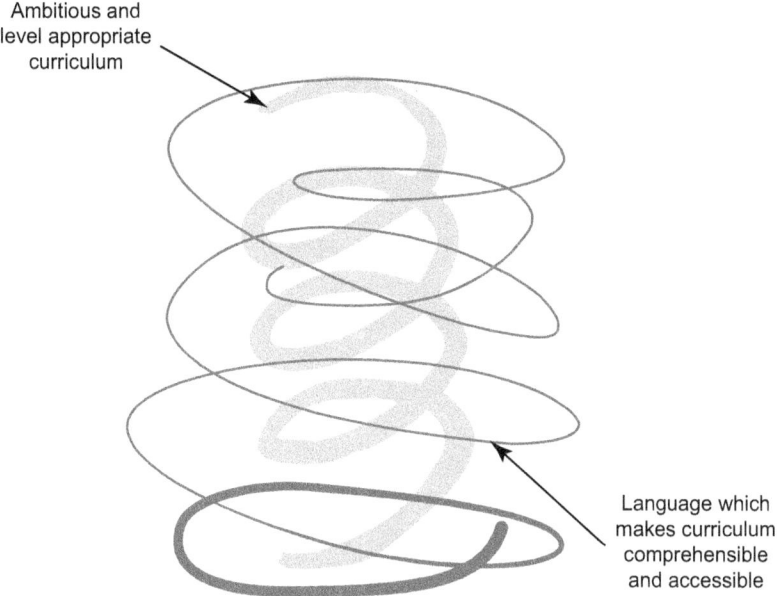

Figure 1.6 What we teach should form the core of our lessons, while how we teach it must be a proactive response to the students in our classroom.

through comprehensible and accessible language, it aids in language development and facilitates their comprehension and engagement with the curriculum. Teaching language and content together enables students to acquire subject-specific vocabulary, grasp complex concepts and participate more fully in classroom discussions. Furthermore, it promotes a holistic understanding of the subject matter, as language is the medium through which ideas and knowledge are conveyed. By integrating language and content instruction, teachers empower EAL learners to navigate the academic world effectively while simultaneously honing their language skills, ensuring a more inclusive and equitable learning experience for all students.

EAL students learn English and learn through English in educational settings where English is the primary language used by the teaching staff and students. Therefore, lessons should be **content-driven**, but everyone involved in lessons should also be **highly language-aware**. This means including all languages, which need to be valued and used for learning and planning for language just as we plan for content, bearing in mind that language learning, like any learning, is an ongoing and lengthy process.

In the contemporary educational landscape, teachers find themselves in a dynamic and multilingual environment. The aim of this book is to provide comprehensive resources for teachers working with EAL and multilingual students, equipping them with practical, classroom-ready tools and activities that can be seamlessly integrated into a variety of subject areas. The focus of this book is to empower educators by offering a repertoire of strategies that celebrate the linguistic and cultural diversity of their students. Throughout the chapters of this book, a wide spectrum of subjects, spanning mathematics, science and the humanities, will be explored. In doing so, the book will present a range of practical activities that can be adapted to various educational contexts and students' English language proficiency levels, enabling teachers to tailor their instruction accordingly.

The organisation of this book is designed to provide a comprehensive approach to language learning, recognising the complexity of language and its multifaceted nature. Each chapter is loosely centred around specific language skills such as reading or writing and the essential components of language such as vocabulary or grammar. It offers in-depth exploration and guidance in these areas. However, it is crucial to remember that language is an intricate web of interconnected elements and neat categorisation often falls short of capturing its richness. Real-world language use does not neatly fit into isolated boxes and this book acknowledges the dynamic and fluid nature of communication. In practice, language skills are frequently interwoven and our lessons reflect this reality by encouraging the simultaneous use of multiple skills. This holistic approach to language learning ensures that students develop a more well-rounded and practical language proficiency, allowing them to effectively navigate the complexities of real-life communication.

Before you prepare any resources or materials, plan a lesson or set an assignment, take the time to look at and analyse the data of your multilingual students, learn about their history and listen to their stories.

References

Cummins, J. 1979. Cognitive/Academic Language Proficiency, Linguistic Interdependence, the Optimum Age Question and Some Other Matters. *Working Papers on Bilingualism*, **19**, pp. 121-129.

Cummins, J. 1984. *Bilingualism and Special Education: Issues in Assessment and Pedagogy*. Clevedon: Multilingual Matters.

Cummins, J. 2021. *Rethinking the Education of Multilingual Learners*. Bristol: Multilingual Matters.

Department for Education. 2020. *English Proficiency of Pupils with English as an Additional Language*. [Online] Accessed 27 July 2023. Available from: https://assets.publishing.service.gov.uk/media/5e55205d86650c10e8754e54/English_proficiency_of_EAL_pupils.pdf.

Department for Education. 2021. *Teachers' Standards*. [Online] Accessed 27 July 2023. Available from: https://assets.publishing.service.gov.uk/media/61b73d6c8fa8f50384489c9a/Teachers__Standards_Dec_2021.pdf.

Demie, F. 2013. English as an Additional Language Pupils: How Long Does It Take to Acquire English Fluency? *Language and Education*, **27**(1), pp. 59-69.

Ellis, R. 2000. *Second Language Acquisition*. Oxford: Oxford University Press.

Foley, Y., Anderson, C., Conteh, J. and Hancock, J. 2018. *Initial Teacher Education and English as an Additional Language*. [Online] Accessed 2 August 2023. Available from: https://www.bell-foundation.org.uk/eal-programme/research/english-as-an-additional-language-and-initial-teacher-education/.

Gibbons, P. 1993. *Learning to Learn in a Second Language*. Portsmouth: Heinemann.

Gibbons, P. 2015. *Scaffolding Language, Scaffolding Learning: Teaching Second Language Learners in Mainstream Classroom*. Portsmouth: Heinemann.

Gonzalez, N. 2005. Beyond Culture: The Hybridity of Funds of Knowledge. In N. Gonzalez, L. C. Moll and C. Amanti, eds. *Funds of Knowledge: Theorizing Practices in Households, Communities and Classrooms*. Mahwah: Lawrence Erlbaum Associates Publishers, pp. 29–46.

Krashen, S. D. 1982. *Principles and Practice in Second Language Acquisition*. Oxford: Pergamon Press.

Krashen, S. D. 1985. *The Input Hypothesis: Issues and Implications*. New York: Longman.

Lightbown, P. M. and Spada, N. 2003. *How Languages are Learned*. Oxford: Oxford University Press.

Polinsky, M. and Kagan, O. 2007. Heritage Languages: In the 'Wild' and in the Classroom. *Language and Linguistics Compass*, **1**(5), pp. 368–395.

Saville-Troike, M. 2006. *Introducing Second Language Acquisition*. Cambridge: Cambridge University Press.

Sharples, R. 2021. *Teaching EAL. Evidence-Based Strategies for the Classroom and School*. Bristol: Multilingual Matters.

Snyder, S and Fenner, S. D. 2021. *Culturally Responsive Teaching for Multilingual Learners. Tools for Equity*. Thousand Oaks: Corwin.

Strand, S. and Hessel, A. 2018. *English as an Additional Language, Proficiency in English and Pupils' Educational Achievement: An Analysis of Local Authority Data*. [Online] Accessed 3 August 2023. Available from: https://www.bell-foundation.org.uk/eal-programme/research/english-as-an-additional-language-proficiency-in-english-and-pupils-educational-achievement-an-analysis-of-local-authority-data/.

Strand, S. and Lindorff, A. 2020. *English as an Additional Language: Proficiency in English, Educational Achievement and Rate of Progression in English Language Learning*. [Online] Accessed 3 August 2023. Available from: https://www.bell-foundation.org.uk/app/uploads/2020/02/University-of-Oxford-Report-Feb-2020-web.pdf.

United Kingdom Statistics Authority. 2023. *Schools, Pupils and Their Characteristics*. [Online] Accessed 12 October 2023. Available from: https://explore-education-statistics.service.gov.uk/find-statistics/school-pupils-and-their-characteristics.

2 Building a strong foundation
Vocabulary development in subject lessons

Once, I was in a conversation with a science teacher and we were discussing a specific class that had many multilingual learners. I cannot recall the exact topic of our conversation – it could have been about the effectiveness of a particular teaching strategy or the upcoming exams. The teacher mentioned that while explaining the law of gravity in one of the lessons, he said, 'If you throw a pebble…' and then proceeded to elaborate on the lesson's subject. A few minutes later, a student raised her hand to ask a question. She inquired, 'Sir, what's a pebble?' At that time, the student had been attending English school for over three years, with more than two years in primary school and several months in secondary school. Her conversational and academic language had been rapidly developing; she could actively participate in all classroom and extracurricular activities. The student's enquiry about the word 'pebble' is, of course, an anecdotal example, but it is likely not far-fetched from the experiences of many multilingual students and their teachers.

Why is vocabulary teaching important?

Effective vocabulary instruction is crucial for the language development of multilingual learners across various academic subjects and social interactions. When we consider the multitude of lessons students attend in a given day, along with the variety of texts they encounter, oral interactions, words and phrases related to studied topics, potential nuanced meanings of each word in different contexts, pronunciation and cultural significance, it becomes apparent that this can be overwhelming for both teachers and students. Questions such as: Which words should be taught? How many in one lesson? Should they be taught explicitly? Will the students be able to understand them from the context of the lesson? Do the students already know these words? Do they recognise them in the context of this specific lesson? are perfectly valid. These also highlight the **significance of systematic and contextually embedded vocabulary instruction** to support ongoing language development among multilingual students.

English language teaching and the emphasis on grammar and vocabulary have undergone various shifts. These changes have been influenced by education theories, linguistic research, technological advancements and a deeper understanding of language acquisition. Teaching multilingual students in content lessons is clearly different from teaching

English as a foreign language but many methodologies have impacted the instruction for multilingual learners. In the early to mid-20th century grammar held a central role. Lessons were structured around grammatical rules and learners were expected to memorise syntactic patterns. Vocabulary was treated as a byproduct of learning and often taught incidentally, mainly as a means to practise the grammatical rules.

The mid-20th century saw a move away from strict grammar-based instruction to more communicative approaches. Emphasis was placed on developing speaking and listening skills for practical communication. Vocabulary teaching became more functional with an emphasis on teaching words and phrases for specific situations and purposes. While still valuing grammatical accuracy, these approaches introduced pattern drilling and repetition for language practice, aiming to develop automaticity in language use.

In the late 20th to early 21st century, language teaching moved further toward communicative and task-based methods, where grammar was taught in context, often through real-world tasks and activities. The importance of vocabulary increased as linguists (for example Michael Lewis) promoted the idea that language is made up of chunks or lexical phrases. With the clear significance of grammar and vocabulary, an approach emerged, emphasising the interconnectedness of these two elements.

Similarly, nowadays, both grammar and vocabulary instructions are encouraged to be taught in a meaningful context. The importance of building a strong and diverse vocabulary to enhance reading comprehension and academic success has been highlighted as a priority (Nagy and Townsend, 2012; Beck, McKeown and Kucan, 2013; Quigley, 2018). The success of reading comprehension, however, is very unlikely to be achieved if students are taught a set of words or are presented with glossaries related to the topic studied in class that, on the surface, are connected to one another but do not contribute to a broader understanding of the context. For instance, when teaching English to beginners during interventions or 'survival English' sessions, introducing ten or more colours in a single lesson might not be the most effective approach. In fact, some research (Tinkham, 1993) suggests that clustering similar words may hinder rather than enhance vocabulary learning. Instead of organising words in semantic clusters (for example, colours, body parts, pieces of furniture, etc.), which may seem helpful for language teaching, it is more effective to adopt a thematic approach that involves grouping words related to a common theme (for example, 'Othello', 'green-eyed', 'monster', 'jealousy', 'suspicion').

Additionally, most primary and secondary school children are already acquainted with many conceptual systems and words to express them, and they can use them as a springboard to create a direct link to the new set of vocabulary (Thornbury, 2002). Research suggests that at lower proficiency levels, words encountered in a new language are closely connected to their equivalents in students' first languages, although some of them might be learned without a direct translation (Nation, 2013). While a lesson on practising colours in English could appear as essential groundwork, it might not present much of a challenge to describe the colours of students' clothing or classroom items. Consequently, students

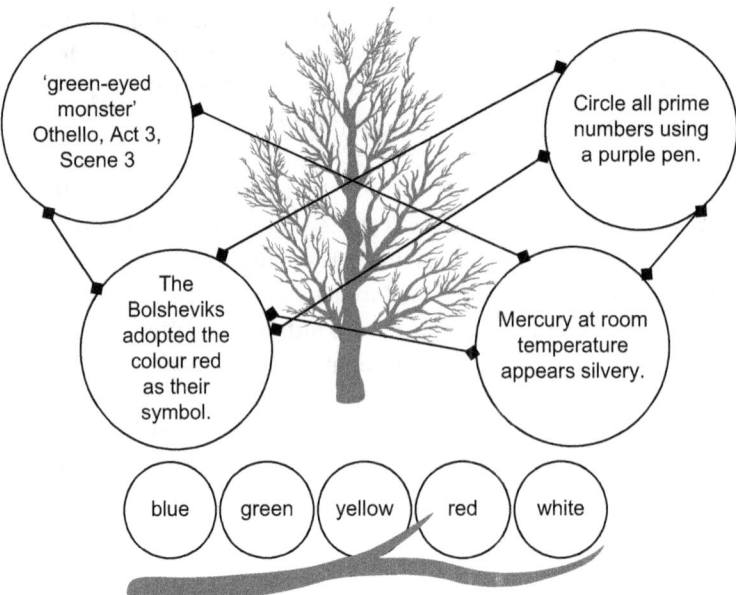

Figure 2.1 Vocabulary is learned more effectively when introduced and practised in meaningful contexts rather than in isolation or as long lists of words.

may perceive very little relevance to the topic and forget the words quickly. Introducing the words within the context of the lesson and exploring their meaning and use in purpose-driven tasks is much more effective. This approach also ensures that all students, regardless of their English language proficiency levels, access content-appropriate lessons.

1, 2, 3, words

Teaching multilingual learners in mainstream classes requires careful consideration and planning with regard to language. Just as a science teacher does not teach 'science' but a very specific concept or a part of a unit during a lesson, it is helpful to look at language as not always teaching the English language but certain elements of it that are connected and realised through the studied topic. With the extremely helpful and influential division of vocabulary into three tiers (Tier 1: everyday, high-frequency vocabulary, Tier 2: academic, cross-disciplinary words, Tier 3: subject-specific terminology) by Beck, McKeown and Kucan in *Bringing Words to Life: Robust Vocabulary Instruction*, we must not forget that for many multilingual (and some monolingual) learners, such a tiered approach should not be treated as a simplified answer to What words do I need to teach?

Effective vocabulary instruction should consider several factors, such as the importance of certain words, their frequency, Tier 2 words, word formation, homonyms and cognates. Most of the examples below will focus on the topic of the Industrial Revolution, but they can be easily adapted for any subject and topic.

Building a strong foundation 31

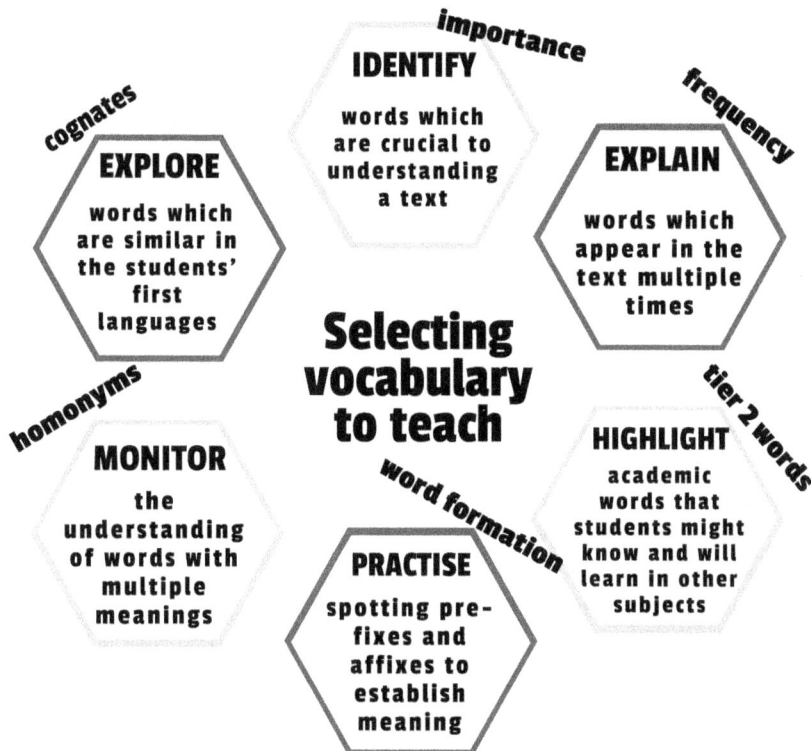

Figure 2.2 There are several factors teachers can consider when choosing vocabulary to be studied and focused on during lessons.

- **The important words:** identify and focus on words pivotal to understanding and engaging with the topic studied. These words and phrases should be taught and revisited over the course of the unit and series of lessons. Many of them will be classified as Tier 3 or subject-specific words, such as 'industrialisation' or trade 'unions'. Some might belong to Tier 1, the more basic and frequently used words, such as 'factory' or 'machines'.
- **The frequent words:** some of these may closely relate to the first category and will appear frequently in texts. You might want to start with basic high-frequency words linked to the topic and gradually introduce less common vocabulary as learners progress in securing their knowledge of the subject. For example, the word 'factory' might be replaced with 'plant', 'industrial unit' or 'production facility'. Many freely available websites allow you to count the number of times each word appears in a text. As expected, articles such as 'a', 'an', 'the', pronouns (e.g., 'it', 'they') and other high-frequency words will appear often. Some words might seem easily comprehensible to students on the surface but have more complex spelling or pronunciation. These words could be highlighted to students and given attention during lessons.
- **Tier 2 words** (more details below): often encountered and essential in academic texts, these words are often not taught explicitly (unlike Tier 3 words) and not as frequently

used in everyday conversations and writing (unlike Tier 1 words). Examples include 'progress' and 'automatic'.

Homonyms: confusing homonyms, words that sound the same but have different meanings (e.g., 'plant' as in a living organism and 'plant' as in an industrial facility), can impede comprehension. It is always a good idea to highlight word meanings in context.

Cognates: recognising cognates, words in two or more languages that share a common origin, typically derived from a common ancestral language, is particularly helpful for multilingual learners. These words often have similar meanings, spelling and pronunciation patterns due to their shared linguistic heritage. Learning about cognates fosters an understanding of the interconnectedness of languages and facilitates vocabulary acquisition. Recognising and understanding cognates help learners expand their vocabulary more quickly and effectively because they can leverage their existing knowledge. For instance, the word 'factory' is very similar across many languages: 'fábrica' in Spanish, 'Fabrik' in German, 'fabrică' in Romanian and 'fabrika' in Slovak. A word of caution: false cognates can be a minor pitfall. These words appear to be cognates due to similar spelling but have different meanings. For example, 'eventually' in English means 'finally' or 'ultimately', but the Polish word 'ewentualnie', although quite similar, is translated as 'alternatively'.

Word formation: understanding word formation rules, roots and affixes (a general term for the elements added to the beginning (prefixes) or end (suffixes) of a base word to change its meaning or create a new word) can help learners decipher the meanings of unfamiliar words. Additionally, it is a valuable skill for deducing the meaning of unknown vocabulary by noticing common patterns. For example, the word 'industrialisation' could be presented and explained to students in the form illustrated in Figure 2.3.

Other words that are very likely to come up during the Industrial Revolution unit, such as 'automatisation', 'mechanisation' or 'urbanisation', follow very similar patterns to which students' attention should be drawn. Spotting affixes and being aware of their roles and meaning will be useful in all subjects, enhancing students' reading comprehension and enabling them to articulate their ideas with greater precision and nuance.

Proactively planning for and pre-empting any unfamiliar or frequently occurring words and phrases in a unit or work might start with a simple table such as in Figure 2.4.

industrial			adjective
industrial	ise		verb
industrial	is	ation	noun
industrialisation			

Figure 2.3 Focusing students' attention on root words as well as their affixes will help students notice patterns and increase their awareness of how some words are created and connect.

Vocabulary Analysis	
Topic: The Industrial Revolution Class: Year 8 **Number of lessons:** 5	
important	industrialisation, textile industry, urbanisation, revolution
frequent	factory, production, transport, to improve, to progress, to invent, to employ, conditions, growth, safety
Tier 2	to innovate, inequality, to transform, significant
word formation	-ation: urbanisation, industrialisation, automation
homonyms	plant, iron
cognates	factory, production, automation

Figure 2.4 Identifying key vocabulary for a unit or a series of lessons ensures that teachers can decide how each word and phrase is going to be practised by students through various activities.

Selecting key vocabulary provides clarity and focus during lessons. Prioritising certain words and expressions, as well as consistently teaching core elements of thematic topics, ensures a strong foundation upon which students can further develop their vocabulary. Categorising words according to their characteristics, as outlined above, can offer a helpful overview of what students need to know in order to understand a lesson, read academic texts, participate in discussions and compose written pieces of work on a given topic. Another possible way to group the vocabulary is by categorising them into the aforementioned tiers: Tier 1, Tier 2 and Tier 3. Teaching and learning these words can be adapted to recognise their features and functions.

Tier 1: the (in)frequent words

Tier 1 words, also known as basic or high-frequency words, are the most common and fundamental words in a language. These words are typically simple, everyday vocabulary that are easily understood and used in everyday communication. They form the foundation of language learning and are essential for effective communication and comprehension.

Characteristics of Tier 1 words include:

- **high frequency:** words are often used in spoken and written language across a variety of contexts.
- **universal relevance:** words are familiar and allow communication for speakers of all ages and language levels, regardless of their background or education.
- **contextually transparent:** these words usually have straightforward meanings that can be understood without requiring much additional context.

- **concrete and familiar concepts:** they often refer to basic objects, actions, feelings and concepts that are part of everyday life.

Tier 1 words are typically among the first that children learn as they acquire language and are essential for building a strong language foundation. They include common, concrete nouns such as 'dog', 'playground' or 'gloves', adjectives like 'tired', 'dirty' and 'tall', verbs related to common actions such as 'run',' 'bring' and 'watch' and prepositions like 'under', 'next to' or 'in'. However, for multilingual learners, some of these words might still be unfamiliar or not commonly used. I once taught a multilingual student in KS4 who was preparing for GCSE exams and could analyse literary pieces using words like 'alliteration', 'to evoke' and 'engrossed', yet she did not know the word for 'spoon'. She used her first language at home with her family and referred to all utensils without using English. In school, there was no need to use the word 'spoon' in any lessons, as she only used a fork and a knife while eating her lunch. As a side note, it is worth mentioning that the mentioned student never attended nursery or classes at KS1, so she was not familiar with many nursery rhymes and stories, which are considered a crucial cultural component of young children's exposure to reading, stories and literature. Once again, this is anecdotal but highlights the non-linearity of language learning and the need to ensure that all students have access to level-appropriate lessons. It also underscores the fact that it is impossible to know exactly which words students are familiar with and which they are not. Tier 1 words are often concrete nouns, verbs that can be explained through simple actions or adjectives that can be illustrated visually. They are often easy to understand based on the context. Multilingual learners, therefore, will learn a significant number of these words implicitly, simply by being exposed to conversations, videos, texts and every interaction in and outside of school. Naturally, though, there will be some words that are not familiar to multilingual learners, especially if they are at A, B or C levels of English language proficiency.

Assigning students responsibility and accountability for unfamiliar words can help alleviate challenges associated with identifying and teaching extensive vocabulary, especially when dealing with Tier 1 common words. Students may be tasked with creating and using flashcards or **word cards** as tools for documenting new words. These personalised cards, if prepared by students, can lead to greater comprehension for individual learners. Lei and Reynolds (2022) concluded that word cards, whether they are digital or in physical form, and whether they are pre-made or created by the learner, can be valuable tools for acquiring vocabulary. They noted that traditional paper word cards may offer advantages compared to their digital counterparts. Similarly, pre-made word cards often perform better than those created by learners themselves. However, this conclusion might be linked to the fact that not all learners are explicitly shown or taught how to compose an effective card and how to use it effectively. This is particularly crucial if students are new to English and are asked to navigate many resources in English and create new ones themselves. The process can also be extremely time-consuming if learners at the initial stages of learning English are asked to use a dictionary either to find a translation or an appropriate definition of a given word. For example, the word 'mouth' features six different entries in the Collins Online Dictionary. Students might end up copying all definitions without being certain of the

Building a strong foundation 35

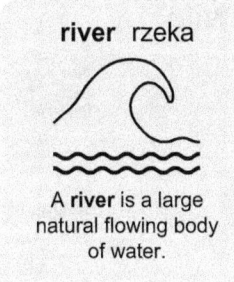 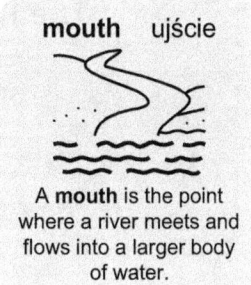

Figure 2.5 Word cards with key words, translation, pictures and definitions.

context in which the word is used or add information that might cloud their understanding and retention of the word (for example, whether the word 'mouth' is countable or uncountable, synonyms of the word 'mouth' used as a verb, etc.). To address these challenges, simple word cards could be provided by the teacher, including the word, a translation (which can be added by a student), a picture or symbol representing the word (particularly useful for abstract concepts) and a definition.

It might be worth considering adding some contextual information so that students can place the definition within a specific situation or context, as illustrated in Figure 2.6, during the study of the River Nile.

Word cards are often favoured by learners at advanced proficiency levels (Lei and Reynolds, 2022) because they have a more secure and nuanced understanding of a wider vocabulary and can more easily distinguish the appropriate definition, form and use of a studied word. Even students at higher levels of English language proficiency will still need guidance on the context in which a word is used if they are tasked with creating their own word cards.

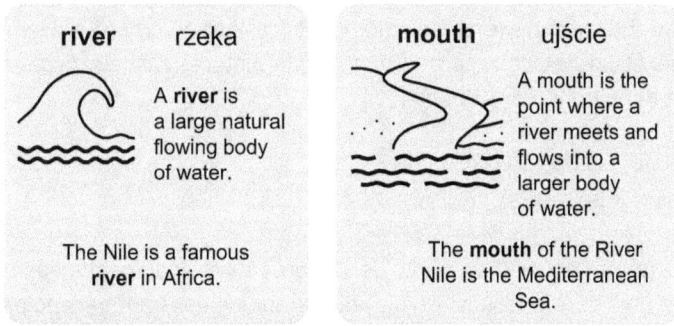

Figure 2.6 Word cards with key words, translation, pictures, definitions and example sentences.

The River Nile

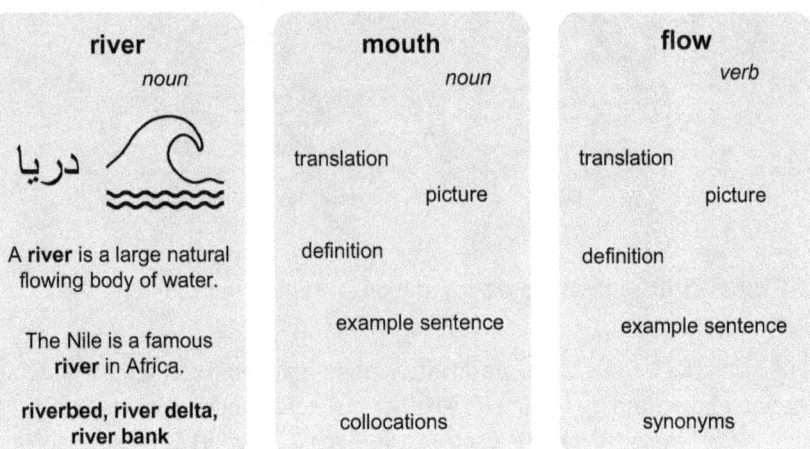

Figure 2.7 Students should be encouraged to produce their own word cards and practise recalling key information independently.

Introducing learners to a large number of new words, which are presented and studied over a relatively short period of time during intense and concentrated study sessions, facilitates repeated encounters with the words. This, in turn, enhances short-term retention and comprehension (Lei and Reynolds, 2022). To promote deep understanding and long-term retention of the material, **spacing out learning over time and reinforcing the material through regular review** is considered a more effective strategy. This strategy can be applied to both Tier 1 and Tier 2 words. Tier 3 words can be studied using the Frayer model, which is discussed later in this chapter.

It would not be possible, nor necessary, to explain every single Tier 1 word on the off chance that some students may not understand it. As teachers, however, we can identify Tier 1 words that are crucial to understanding the overall message of a text or explanation, or that will be repeated and used in a lesson on multiple occasions and therefore it might be worth explaining. This could be achieved by using simple pictures, visuals, gestures, synonyms and very short definitions. For example:

If I throw a pebble, or a small rock…
If I throw a pebble…

It is important to remember that many Tier 1 words have additional meanings in various contexts or are part of expressions where understanding does not depend on the comprehension of each element separately. For example, phrases such as 'head start', 'to chair a meeting' or 'turn the tables' might be quite confusing, and students will likely benefit from a more explicit explanation.

Figure 2.8 Visuals may help establish the meaning of some concrete words. Created by Gan Khoon Lay from Noun Project.

Tier 2: the universal words

Tier 2 words, also known as academic vocabulary, refer to words that are more sophisticated and less commonly used in everyday language compared to basic Tier 1 words. These words are essential for understanding and expressing complex ideas, both in written and spoken communication. Tier 2 words often appear across a range of academic disciplines and are crucial for academic success, for example: 'incorporate', 'framework' or 'diminish'. Many words referred to as Tier 2 vocabulary form part of the Academic Word List (AWL) developed by Dr Coxhead in 2000 which consists of 570 word families that are commonly found in academic texts across various disciplines (Coxhead, 2000). The AWL is divided into ten sublists, each containing approximately 60 word families. These words are chosen on their frequency in academic texts and their relevance to a wide range of disciplines.

Tier 2 words are typically characterised by the following features:

- **general applicability:** Tier 2 words are usually relevant and useful across a variety of subjects and contexts. They are not necessarily limited to specific topics or areas of study.
- **rich meaning**: these words have multiple meanings, shades of meaning or nuanced connotations. They add depth and precision to communication.
- **contextual dependence:** the meanings of Tier 2 words can be inferred from the context in which they are used, making them crucial for reading comprehension.

- **frequency of use**: while Tier 2 words are less common than basic Tier 1 words, they still appear frequently in academic texts, literature and academic discussions.
- **critical for academic success**: proficiency in Tier 2 words is important for achieving higher levels of literacy and effective communication in educational and professional settings.

The AWL is often used as a resource for language learners, educators and researchers to enhance vocabulary development. However, it has been noted that, although we refer to academic words as cross-disciplinary, they do change their nuanced meaning when used in different subjects (Gardner and Davies, 2014). For example, if the word 'react' is taught explicitly in a science lesson, it would be too risky to assume that we can use the word 'react' in a history lesson without providing a historical context. In a history lesson, 'react' could be used to describe how people or nations responded to a particular event or situation. For example,

> The citizens' protests were a natural reaction to the oppressive policies.

Whereas in a science lesson, 'react' is more likely to refer to a chemical reaction, where substances interact to produce new compounds:

> When hydrogen and oxygen gases react in the presence of a catalyst, they form water.

Intentional vocabulary learning is a more structured approach to acquiring new words and expanding students' vocabulary. Unlike incidental learning, which is unplanned and less controlled, intentional vocabulary learning is systematic, with teachers and learners selecting words based on their relevance to the curriculum. An analysis that summarised results from 22 primary studies concluded that intentional vocabulary learning leads to greater gains than incidental learning (Webb, Yanagisawa and Uchihara, 2000). It also states that students need to encounter a particular word on multiple occasions to ensure they can recall both its form and its meaning. Learners' attention should be actively drawn to key words and expressions, and they should be provided with opportunities to reuse and recall newly introduced words.

Developing a unified approach to teaching academic vocabulary explicitly across various disciplines can enable **a systematic and well-embedded approach** to expanding students' depth and range of lexicon. Research confirms that the proposed five-step process used at Trinity Academy Leeds ensures that all teachers are confident in how to introduce each component of an academic word: pronunciation, form, use and meaning (adapted from Beck, McKeown and Kucan, 2013).

The script below is an example of how the depth and a particular context of the word 'react' might be explored during a history lesson. It would probably be safe to assume that many or most students, including multilingual learners, will be familiar with the word 'react'. They

Building a strong foundation 39

Figure 2.9 The five-step model to introduce and practise key academic vocabulary.

might have used it in an everyday context or an academic one, for example, in science. The purpose of this activity is to ensure that the students can understand and use the word in a more nuanced way. This is how this stage of the lesson can proceed:

Step 1: I say, you say

> The word which we will take a closer look at is 'react'. 'React'. I say 'react', you say _____ .

This is when the whole class repeats the word chorally. At this stage, students practise the pronunciation as a group; nobody is singled out, so it is a safe, non-threatening way. It is usually repeated two or three times, or if a word is long and difficult to pronounce, the word might be broken down into easily manageable syllables. Once the students have practised saying the word a couple of times, the teacher might decide to focus on a particular group or a student, either to model for the rest of the class or to allow for further practice:

> I say 'react', the first row says _____ .
> I say 'react', Mario says _____ .

Step 2: define it

> The word 'react' is a verb. What is a verb? Can you define the word 'verb'?

It is not required for teachers to know, explain in detail or cite the grammar rules, but the shared metalanguage allows one to observe how, in this case, parts of speech 'behave' and change in different sentences.

> Yes, verbs refer to actions or states. The word 'react' is a verb. When you react to something that has happened to you, you behave in a particular way because of it. To react to something means to behave.

Step 3: use it in a sentence

During the next stage, a teacher provides an example sentence with the new word. It does not have to be an example connected to or directly related to the lesson at this stage. If it describes situations with which students are familiar in everyday scenarios, it might be easier for them to understand what the word means. The example sentence might be:

> When I told her the news, she didn't **react** immediately, but after a moment of silence, she burst into tears.

If time allows, a couple of minutes might be spent focusing on the sentence and asking students questions so that they can practise the key verb in different forms and notice how other parts of speech are created:

> Why do you think she reacted this way?
> What might have caused the woman's reaction?

Step 4: turn and talk

Step 4 allows for more independent practice and can be done in pairs, small groups or independently. The students might be provided with a visual, a drawing or a picture illustrating a certain situation and asked a question or be provided with a statement, for example:

> How do you typically **react** in high-stress situations?
> How do you **react** when you receive a challenging task or a difficult test at school?
> Has it always been your **reaction**?

While discussing the answers, the students have to use the key word. At this stage, we are looking for short and succinct answers, so 20–30 seconds per student, if working in pairs, should be enough. The teacher might ask a couple of students to share their answers in the class forum.

Step 5: 3, 2, 1 whiteboards

The last stage involves a very brief writing activity for which the use of mini whiteboards might be effective. Students are asked to write their one-sentence answers that they have been discussing with their peers. This activity allows students to practise spelling, focus on punctuation, syntax and the order of words in a sentence. The teacher can quickly check for any emerging patterns that might need addressing while the students write the sentences, and then have them hold their mini-whiteboards up in the air.

Tier 3: the domain-specific words

Tier 3 words, often referred to as 'subject' or 'domain-specific' vocabulary, are words that are not commonly used in everyday conversation but are essential for understanding specific subjects or fields of study. These words typically have precise meanings and are specific to particular disciplines or topics.

The key characteristics of Tier 3 words:

- **precision:** these words have precise and well-defined meanings within their respective domains. Their meanings are often not easily inferred without prior knowledge of the subject matter.
- **context-dependent:** the meaning of Tier 3 words can vary based on the context in which they are used. Understanding the context is essential for correctly interpreting these words.
- **technical or scientific:** many Tier 3 words are technical, scientific or jargon specific to a particular field. They may involve complex concepts or processes.
- **necessary for comprehension:** in academic or professional contexts, Tier 3 words are essential for reading comprehension and effective communication within a specific field. Without a grasp of these words, it can be challenging to understand and engage with subject-specific texts or discussions.
- **limited general use:** Tier 3 words are typically not used in general conversations or writing. Instead, they are reserved for discussions and writings within their respective domains.
- **subject variability:** similar to some Tier 2 words, the specific Tier 3 words can vary depending on the field or discipline.
- **key to domain mastery:** in many cases, mastery of Tier 3 vocabulary is necessary to excel in a particular field of study. Proficiency in these words demonstrates a deep understanding of the subject matter.
- **formal and academic registers:** these words are often used in formal and academic registers, such as textbooks, research papers, technical manuals and academic or professional presentations.
- **challenging for learners:** Tier 3 words can be challenging for learners, especially those who are new to a specific domain. These words might be as challenging to monolingual as to multilingual learners as they often represent and refer to complex, multi-staged processes.

The five-step process for introducing and practising Tier 2 vocabulary is not effective when dealing with Tier 3 words. Tier 3 words are essential to a particular subject or domain; therefore, it is highly unlikely that students will be able to use unknown words such as 'topography', 'feudalism' or 'mitosis' during the first or even the second lesson. Although it is possible to provide simple and succinct definitions of these words, it is more likely that students will need to understand the meaning of these words in a specific context, which is much more complex and underpinned by knowledge of interconnected ideas than a one-sentence explanation.

The **Frayer model**, developed in the 1960s by Dorothy Frayer and her colleagues at the University of Wisconsin, is a **graphic organiser** that helps students explore and understand the meaning of not only words but also concepts in a structured way. It is a versatile tool and can be adapted depending on the topic, complexity of the concepts or the students' background knowledge and English language proficiency levels. In its most straightforward version, the model encourages students to think about a word's definitions, characteristics, examples and non-examples. In the definition section, students write down the definition of the word. It can be the dictionary definition, but it might be more effective if students are asked to write a simplified explanation of the word in their own words. This step ensures that students grasp the core definition of the word. Next, students identify the essential characteristics, attributes or qualities associated with the word or concept. They can think about what the word represents, its important features and how it fits into a broader context. In the example section, students provide examples of how the word is used in sentences. These examples should illustrate the word's meaning in context. Students can write a list of examples or create sentences that accurately showcase the word's usage. Finally, the non-example is a part of the model where students list situations, sentences or contexts in which the word would not be appropriate or applicable. Non-examples help clarify the word's limitations and where it does not fit.

A completed Frayer model might look like Figure 2.10.

There are many variations of the model, with some additional sections which might include: a visual representation of the word, translation into students' first languages, synonyms and antonyms (avoid including unfamiliar or not well-established words as it might be unhelpful and cause confusion), etymology of the word and its root word, prefixes and suffixes creating different parts of speech.

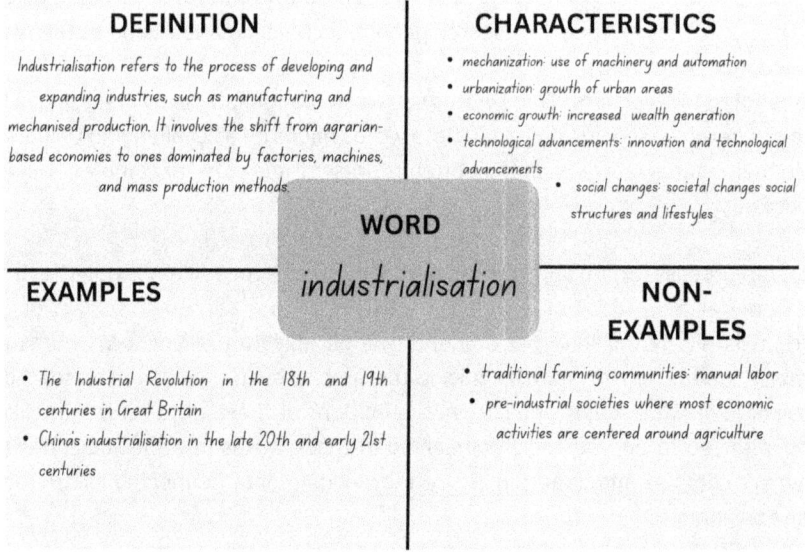

Figure 2.10 The Frayer model allows the practice of key vocabulary related to concepts studied in a variety of subjects.

Building a strong foundation 43

DEFINITION	WORD	PICTURE + MY LANGUAGE
Industrialisation is the process of reducing/expanding industries, such as manufacturing and mechanised/manual production. Economies are dominated by factories and machines.	*industrialisation* in-dus-tri-al-iz-a-tion in , dustriali ' sation noun	[factory icon] *iparositas*
CHARACTERISTICS • m_ch_n_z_t_ _n: use of machinery and automation • _rb_n_z_t_ _n: growth of urban areas • e_____ g_____: increased wealth generation • t_____ a_____: innovation and technological advancements	industry + isation from 'industria' suffix used which means to create 'skills', 'diligence' nouns to or 'activity indicate a process **to industrialise** **(verb)** **industrial (adjective)**	**EXAMPLES ✓** **NON-EXAMPLES ✗** __The Industrial Revolution in the 18th and 19th centuries in Great Britain __traditional farming communities: manual labor __China's industrialisation in the late 20th and early 21st centuries

Figure 2.11 The Frayer model is easily adaptable; further study of key vocabulary, its roots, affixes and etymology can be added to deepen students' understanding of key words.

The example in Figure 2.11 features the word broken into syllables, which might help students with spelling and sounding the word out. The places of stress are indicated in the next line, which will also allow students to practise the pronunciation of the word. Knowing the part of speech, which is named next, might assist students with the appropriate use in sentences. Furthermore, there is a focus on etymology, and the word is broken into two meaningful parts. Each of these parts, derived from Latin, enables students to start making connections between the roots and suffixes that they are already familiar with.

Although the 'definition', 'characteristics' and 'examples and non-examples' sections are very similar to the previous ones, they could be pre-populated before the lesson. This might assist students who are still developing their competence in engaging with the vocabulary used during the topic. In the 'definition' part, students are asked to choose one of the words so that the explanation is correct. Similarly, in the 'characteristics' section, they are provided with the definitions and tasked with providing the words – scaffolding is provided in the form of some first letters and fill-gap words. Moreover, students can tick or cross examples and non-examples so that their understanding can be checked. The 'pictures + my language' part can be completed by a student independently. The whole activity might be repeated a couple of lessons later or at the end of the topic but will have less or no scaffolding to gauge if the students' understanding of the notion has been established and if they have acquired the necessary vocabulary to explain it.

44 Building a strong foundation

The Frayer model and the systematic and structured approach to introducing new words are beneficial to all students, but for multilingual learners, in particular, it helps students grasp the meaning and context of words more effectively. Since the model goes beyond simple word translations or brief definitions, it encourages students to think deeply about the concept or meaning behind a word. Therefore, it promotes a thorough **understanding of the word's usage and nuances**. Additionally, this approach allows students to see words in sentences, providing valuable **context for how the word is applied**. Multilingual learners can also draw on their knowledge of one language when learning another as the activity can help students identify similarities and differences between the words in their first languages.

Similarly to Figure 2.5, teachers might want to identify key vocabulary before teaching a particular unit to have an overview of the pivotal words, or they could do it on a lesson-to-lesson basis. The lesson-to-lesson approach might be more responsive to students' levels and account for certain words being practised more often than others or, indeed, being added after each lesson if initially they have not been identified as potentially unknown to students.

All words are important

As mentioned earlier, it is quite difficult to know which words are or might be familiar to students at different proficiency levels. Similarly, it might be confusing and challenging for students to **identify or prioritise learning the words and phrases** that will allow them to understand and access the lessons. Trying to remember and learn all new words in a given lesson or even a school day presents a huge cognitive load and might make students feel overwhelmed. Colour-coding or using a system that allows teachers and students to distinguish each tiered word might help one to see the relative importance and frequency

Topic: The Industrial Revolution	Class: Year 8	Lesson 1
Tier 3	industrialisation, urbanisation, society	
Tier 2	to develop, to innovate, significant, to alter	
Tier 1	factory, worker, growth	

Topic: The Industrial Revolution	Class: Year 8	Lesson 2
Tier 3	industrialisation, urbanisation,	
Tier 2	to innovate, to alter, to transform	
Tier 1	coal, goods, handmade	

Figure 2.12 Identifying key vocabulary in each tier might support teachers with a systematic and structured approach to vocabulary teaching in mainstream lessons.

of words in a text or glossaries. For example, if key Tier 1 words are highlighted in a text, learners can quickly realise that these are high-frequency words and likely essential for comprehension. This might aid in understanding the text as a whole. If Tier 2 words, which will be encountered in other subjects, are highlighted, it might help learners understand the different contexts in which a word is used. Identifying key subject-specific words will ensure that these 'low-frequency' and not essential for everyday communication words are prioritised. They are crucial for understanding specific academic texts and are used in particular contexts.

It is important to note that it is not about classifying all words and circling, underlining or colour-coding the entire passages. It is about being intentional and strategic while drawing students' attention to the words, phrases and expressions needed to understand the topic, which are featured in written text and required for students to use in subsequent lessons. A teacher can model how to choose key vocabulary or explicitly state which words and phrases are pivotal for students to understand, remember and actively use during either spoken or written activities. For example:

> **The Industrial Revolution** in England, which <u>unfolded (or lasted)</u> from the late 18th to early 19th centuries, represents <u>a pivotal moment</u> (or important moment) in history. It brought about <u>a profound shift (or a significant change)</u> in how **society** (or people and communities) operated, fundamentally <u>altering</u> (or changing) the economic and technological landscape.

The words in brackets could be explained verbally or added as annotations during the lesson. The passage could also be modified in advance:

> **The Industrial Revolution** in England, which <u>unfolded</u> from the late 18th to early 19th centuries, represents <u>a pivotal moment</u> in history. It brought about <u>a profound shift</u> in how **society** operated, fundamentally <u>altering</u> the economic and technological landscape.
>
> Prior to **the Industrial Revolution,** most goods were crafted by hand, but the advent of game-changing **inventions** such as **the spinning jenny** and **the steam engine** ushered in a new era. These **innovations** paved the way for the establishment of **factories** and the rapid **growth of cities**.
>
> However, it was not without its <u>drawbacks</u>. The surge in factory work led to challenging labour conditions, extended **working hours** and social disparities. Additionally, the rapid **industrialisation** had <u>adverse effects</u> on **the environment**, contributing to pollution and other ecological concerns.

The key expressions, when written down, provide the very essence of the three paragraphs above.

46 *Building a strong foundation*

> The Industrial Revolution – a pivotal moment – a profound shift – altering – society
>
> the Industrial Revolution – inventions – the spinning jenny – the steam engine – innovations – factories – the growth of cities
>
> drawbacks – the industrialisation – working hours – adverse effects – the environment

Using the word and phrase bank above, students might be asked to recreate the sentences. They do not have to be identical to the original ones, but the writing should reflect the key message of each paragraph, for example:

> The Industrial Revolution was a pivotal moment in history. It brought a profound shift altering the way society operated.

If the colours or the way the key words are distinguished as pivotal are used consistently in lessons, students will routinely recognise them as crucial to the overall understanding of the text. With practice and time, students can become skilled at choosing the vocabulary they are not familiar with, recording it and noting down the meaning. This would be particularly useful for more frequently used words, which might be unknown to learners yet not explained or translated due to time restrictions or the assumption that they are already part of the students' linguistic repertoire. It is important for students to take **responsibility for identifying and recording key vocabulary and phrases**. It might be effective for students to start building their own word banks and glossaries from the very first lesson when a topic is introduced. To start with, the teacher could choose four to five items per lesson and ask students to record them in the table as suggested in Figure 2.13.

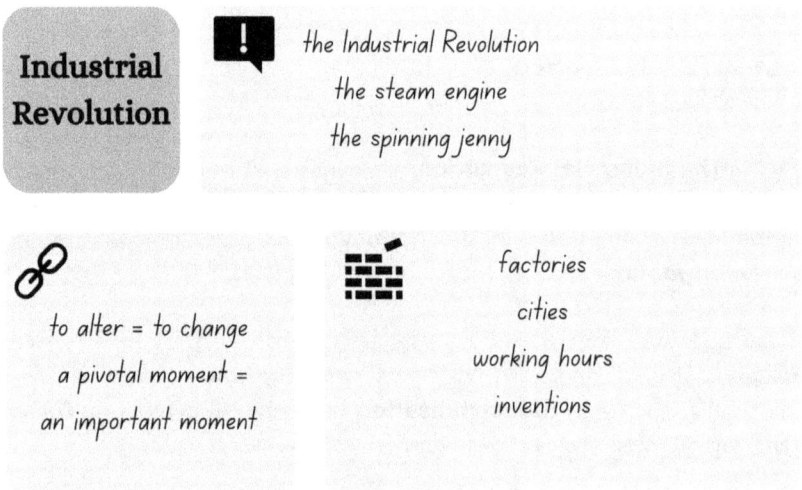

Figure 2.13 Keeping notes of key words and phrases can encourage students to look for connections between the words they already know and allows them to create a personalised record of important vocabulary.

The three distinct parts represent the three-tiered vocabulary. The first one is reserved for subject-specific words and phrases that are crucial for students to discuss a topic with a certain level of expertise. Although the last section is reserved for more common or frequently used words, it is still evident that these are interconnected and form the basis of lexical cohesion – these are the building blocks without which students will not be able to discuss the topic. The middle part, represented by the linked chain, signifies vocabulary that connects the ideas into a coherent text. Additionally, it can be applied across various disciplines.

Although, to start with, the teacher might want to guide students towards key vocabulary, later on, students should be in the habit of recording important or new vocabulary either throughout the lesson or as they come across an unknown word. They could be encouraged to add a translation, a visual or a short definition or a synonym. This will allow them to create their own personalised glossaries and serve as a valuable source of subject-specific vocabulary during longer, independent written tasks.

Beyond single words

Knowing a language and being able to use it proficiently goes beyond memorising and understanding the meaning of individual words. While understanding the meaning of a given word is crucial, each word may have multiple forms (for example, the verb 'take' changes into 'took', 'taken', 'taking', just to name a few). Furthermore, a word's meaning can vary depending on the context and situation, and due to complex social interactions, the **interpretation of words is a multi-layered process**. Additionally, simply knowing words does not guarantee the ability to construct grammatically appropriate sentences and longer passages. Language is often viewed not as single words but as groups of words.

These 'sequences of two or more words that operate as single units' are defined as **collocations** (Thornbury, 2006: 36) and are strongly associated with The Lexical Approach, which gained popularity in the 1990s. Collocations are combinations of words that frequently and naturally occur together in a language. Often, these combinations are considered typical and idiomatic, having a specific meaning that may not be directly derived from the individual meanings of the words. For example, when describing coffee's taste or potency, we use the collocation 'strong coffee', not 'powerful coffee' or 'intense coffee'. Similarly, it is the verb 'make' that collocates with 'decision', not 'create' or 'do'. While these examples illustrate the habitual and natural pairing of words or terms, some linguists suggest drawing students' attention to words that they 'would not expect to see together' (Woolard, 2000: 29) to identify unusual lexical collocations. For instance, the collocation 'a nuclear family' is less likely to be understood by students than 'a nuclear bomb'.

Firstly, learning collocations is beneficial for multilingual students, particularly at levels A to C, as acquiring **prefabricated chunks** of language alleviates the need to understand all the grammatical components governing a particular expression (Hill, 2000; Nation, 2008). Since learners retrieve lexical phrases rather than individual words from their long-term memory, their speech becomes more fluent, natural and idiomatic. This often leads to higher levels of proficiency (McCarthy and O'Dell, 2017; Thornbury, 2006). Secondly, it expands learners' vocabulary, allowing them to be both expressive (McCarthy and O'Dell, 2017) and precise in their descriptions by avoiding long, vague and open-to-interpretation explanations (Woolard, 2000). Hyland (Hyland, 2003) emphasises the significance of accuracy and precision that second language learners need to achieve, particularly in writing. Unlike speaking, writing does not typically happen in real-time conditions and cannot be revised for clarity later. This is a crucial factor to consider, as many exams are either conducted in written form or include substantial written components.

To address the issue of focusing on individual words rather than collocations and the abundance of collocations in lessons, teachers need to consciously decide to include the teaching or at least awareness of collocations. The concept of noticing in language learning has been extensively discussed and researched by Richard Schmidt, an influential linguist and researcher. He is credited with developing the **noticing hypothesis** as a fundamental component of second language acquisition theory. The noticing hypothesis suggests that in order to learn a new language, learners must consciously notice linguistic features or aspects of the language input. In other words, learners need to pay attention to the language features they encounter in the input to facilitate the process of language acquisition (Schmidt, 1990).

To proficient users, collocations are intuitive, but for language learners, the sheer number of collocations can be overwhelming. Therefore, it is important to identify these either before the lesson or make them explicit to students during classroom activities to heighten their awareness of these lexical items. The teacher could simply highlight or circle the expressions rather than treat them as separate words. If we look at the text below, we will notice that the expressions in bold make sense because they appear together and form a lexical unit. If we were to remove one of the words, for example, 'pivotal' from the expression 'pivotal moment', the sentence loses its clarity. The absence of the word 'major' from the phrase 'major changes' does not negatively affect readers' understanding of the text, but it does, however, strip it of its depth and nuanced perception of something important.

> The Industrial Revolution, which started in the late 1700s, was **a pivotal moment** in history because it brought about **major changes**. It shifted societies from relying on farming and **handmade goods** to using machines and factories. This shift led to big **technological advances**, cities growing larger and more jobs in factories.

There are many online collocation dictionaries that provide information about word combinations, grammatical patterns and example sentences. Helpfully, the words are often grouped in a way that allows users to expand their vocabulary and use a variety of synonyms correctly. For example, the word 'pivotal' in the expression 'pivotal moment' can be replaced by 'critical', 'crucial', 'decisive', 'important' or 'key'. Highlighting, drawing students' attention to and encouraging them to record collocations, rather than single words

Building a strong foundation 49

(as shown above), will allow them to achieve efficiency and precision in spoken and written discourses.

Other activities focusing on practising collocations might include providing students with longer and grammatically more complex definitions of key collocations. Students have to recall the phrases and then use them in writing, for example, by answering a question based on the topic being studied. This strategy (adapted from Conzett, 2000) ensures that students are provided with some guidance on the most frequently used collocations. It narrows down the collocations by theme, as they are generated by the content studied in lessons, and allows for multiple exposures, increasing retention by students.

This strategy is particularly effective if students are encouraged not only to activate their knowledge of collocations but also to use them actively in writing. Many students can recall expressions correctly but struggle to use them at the sentence level. To ensure that the task yields good results, students must integrate them into written passages, such as the one below:

> ***Romeo and Juliet*** is a tragic love story set in Verona. It centres around the deep love between two young people who are members of two patriarchal families involved in a long-standing feud. Their forbidden relationship leads to a series of tragic events.

someone who provides support and helps someone. They are dedicated, reliable and trustworthy	long-lasting feud
severe, destructive and far reaching results that have a profound negative impact	patriarchal family
a romantic or intimate connection between individuals that prohibited or seen as unacceptable	faithful companion
a one sided romantic relationship where only one person has strong feeling for another person	unrequited love
a bitter conflict of disagreement between individuals or groups that extends over a significant period of time	forbidden relationship
a family system in which male members hold primary authority and power	deep love
intense affection or emotional affection between individuals	devastating consequences

Figure 2.14 One of the activities focusing on students' vocabulary development might be matching collocations and their explanations.

Drawing students' attention to phrases rather than single words could also include translating collocations and idiomatic expressions into students' first languages. Since collocations and idioms often have **figurative or culturally specific meanings**, translating them into students' first languages can help clarify the intended meaning, making it easier for learners to understand and use these expressions correctly. For example, for most learners, the first association of the word 'heavy' might be related to 'weight' rather than 'density' or 'thickness'. Translating the phrases into their first languages might draw students' attention to the similarities and differences between English and other languages. In many languages, the word 'strong', in literal translation, is used instead of 'heavy'. The resemblance in vocabulary and grammar between the first and the second languages can aid in the comprehension of the second language. When the distinctions between the two languages are minor, learners can use their knowledge of common words shared by both languages to understand the lexical items in the new language by utilising all their linguistic resources (Zhang and Zhang, 2020). Translating can also aid in retention and memorisation and allows students to establish connections between words and concepts in their first languages.

Translating phrases and expressions, such as idioms or collocations, allows students to use all their linguistic repertoire to draw connections between the languages or notice the differences.

The role of noticing and its importance in a single vocabulary item and grammar learning, which were mentioned earlier, applies to learning collocations. According to Conzett (2000), the act of noticing helps learners grasp the various collocation patterns and allows them to transfer this newfound knowledge to enhance their understanding as well as their productive skills. Lewis (2000) explains that noticing happens in two distinct ways: one when we deliberately pay attention to something, and two when we unintentionally become aware of it. Therefore, there are two types of noticing that can be beneficial for acquiring collocations: the one that takes place when students are exposed to spoken discourse, such

How do you say 'heavy rain' in your language?

What's the meaning of the word 'heavy' in the phrase 'heavy rain'?

What word do you use in your language instead of the word 'heavy'?

Figure 2.15 Translating phrases and expressions, such as idioms or collocations, allows students to use all their linguistic repertoire to draw connections between the languages or notice the differences.

Building a strong foundation 51

as discussions, explanations or texts read aloud to them or the written ones during which they encounter the same patterns and phrases on multiple occasions. The other one is a more deliberate task and might be orchestrated by a teacher and integrated into the lesson or independent work. A simple and straightforward activity, which potentially could yield very good results in students' oral and written answers, might be noticing and noting down key collocations (in the example below, adjective-noun patterns) while reading a text.

Earth, a spherical planet, is approximately 4.5 billion years old, residing within the solar system as the third celestial body from the Sun. Its atmosphere comprises vital gases, creating a life-sustaining environment. The Earth's diverse ecosystems support a multitude of species. Geological features like continents, oceans and tectonic plates shape its surface. Gravity, a fundamental force, maintains Earth's orbital path. Its axial tilt gives rise to seasons, influencing climate patterns. Earth's dynamic geological processes continuously transform its landscape.

adjective	noun
_____	system
_____	body
_____	gases
_____	environment
_____	_____
_____	_____

Students should be encouraged to use the identified phrases in their answers, transitioning from merely noticing the language to actively employing it, in order to achieve accuracy and precision in their responses.

Vocabulary knowledge, whether a student is monolingual or multilingual, is an aspect of language that continues to develop and deepen as students progress through their school years. Everyday frequently used words and phrases are learned and mastered relatively quickly and easily, as outlined above, and are referred to as conversational fluency. While many words are learned incidentally through available context, often physical or visual, during face-to-face interactions, others require a more systematic and structured approach. The former occur regularly, are usually highly predictable and can be somewhat repetitive to a certain degree (Gibbons, 2015). In contrast, the latter are often acquired through reading various texts, listening and participating in everyday classroom interactions and discussions. When learners are exposed to lexically dense and complex written texts, as well as spoken explanations and discussions in the classroom environment, they are tasked with comprehending and remembering many low-frequency and technical words. Therefore, some vocabulary should be acquired through regular and planned activities that **focus on explicit vocabulary teaching**, which is necessary to access and produce academic texts. These activities benefit not only multilingual learners but are also extremely advantageous for all students.

Summary

Why?

- **comprehension:** a broad vocabulary range is essential for understanding spoken and written language. Multilingual learners need to acquire a substantial vocabulary to comprehend what they hear and read in the classroom and beyond.
- **communication:** vocabulary forms the foundation of effective communication. Multilingual learners need to acquire diverse vocabulary to express themselves more precisely and effectively in English, which is essential for both academic and social interactions.
- **academic success:** learning in a mainstream educational setting exposes multilingual learners to specific vocabulary in various subjects. An extensive vocabulary helps them excel in their studies.
- **reading proficiency:** reading comprehension highly depends on vocabulary knowledge. A larger vocabulary allows multilingual learners to read more advanced texts and engage with a broader range of literature and academic materials.
- **writing skills:** vocabulary is crucial for effective writing. Multilingual learners who can draw from a wide and diverse vocabulary can write more coherent, precise and well-structured responses.

How?

1. select and analyse the vocabulary that students will need to know in order to understand and engage with a lesson or unit.
2. identify key vocabulary and determine how it will be introduced and explained to students: using pictures, oral explanations, incidental learning (students will understand it based on context and repeated exposure), explicit vocabulary teaching or context-focused vocabulary learning (such as the use of the Frayer model).
3. encourage students to take ownership of their learning by modelling and explaining how they might record new vocabulary using various methods, such as word cards or word banks.
4. teach both single lexical units, such as words, and multiword expressions, such as collocations, fixed phrases or idioms.
5. ensure you explain any cultural references associated with the studied words.
6. plan and incorporate activities that are content- and context-based and include key vocabulary.

Levels

A-E:

Vocabulary development should occur continuously throughout students' entire time at school.

This should be achieved through carefully planned activities as well as incidental learning.

References

Beck, I. L., McKeown, M. G. and Kucan, L. 2013. *Bringing Words to Life: Robust Vocabulary Instruction*. New York: Guildford.

Coxhead, A. 2000. A New Academic Word List. *TESOL Quarterly*, **34**(2), pp. 213-238.

Collins Online Dictionary. [Online] Accessed 22 July 2023. Available from: www.collinsdictionary.com.

Conzett, J. 2000. Integrating Collocation into a Reading and Writing Course. In M. Lewis, ed. *Teaching Collocation: Further Developments in the Lexical Approach*. Hove: Language Teaching Publications, pp. 70-87.

Gardner, D. and Davies, M. 2014. A New Academic Vocabulary List. *Applied Linguistics*, **35**(3), pp. 305-327.

Gibbons, P. 2015. *Scaffolding Language, Scaffolding Learning: Teaching Second Language Learners in Mainstream Classroom*. Portsmouth: Heinmann.

Hill, J. 2000. Revising Priorities: From Grammatical Failure to Collocational Success. In M. Lewis, ed. *Teaching Collocation: Further Developments in the Lexical Approach*. Hove: Language Teaching Publications, pp. 47-69.

Hyland, K. 2003. *Second Language Writing*. Cambridge: Cambridge University Press.

Lei, Y. and Reynolds, B. L. 2022. Learning English Vocabulary from Word Cards: A Research Synthesis. *Frontiers in Psychology*, **13**, pp. 1-26.

Lewis, M. 1993. *The Lexical Approach*. Hove: Language Teaching Publications.

McCarthy, M & O'Dell, F. 2017. *Collocations in Use. Intermediate*. Cambridge: Cambridge University Press.

Nagy, W. and Townsend, D. 2012. Words as Tools: Learning Academic Vocabulary as Language Acquisition. *Reading Research Quarterly*, **47**, pp. 91-108.

Nation, I. S. P. 2013. *Learning Vocabulary in Another Language* (2nd ed.). Cambridge: Cambridge University Press.

Online Collocation Dictionary. [Online] Accessed 15 August 2023. Available from: www.freecollocation.com.

Quigley, A. 2018. *Closing Vocabulary Gap*. Oxon: Routledge.

Schmidt, R. 1990. The Role of Consciousness in Second Language Learning. *Applied Linguistics*, **11**, pp. 129-158.

Thornbury, S. 2006. *How to Teach Vocabulary?* Harlow: Pearson Education Limited.

Tinkham, T. 1993. The Effect of Semantic Clustering on the Learning of Second Language Vocabulary. *System*, **21**, pp. 371-389.

Webb, S., Yanagisawa, A. and Uchihara, T. 2000. How Effective Are Intentional Vocabulary-Learning Activities? *The Modern Language Journal*, **104**(5), pp. 715-738.

Woolard, G. 2000. Collocation: Encouraging Learner Independence. In M. Lewis, ed. *Teaching Collocation: Further Developments in the Lexical Approach*. Hove: Language Teaching Publications, pp. 28-46.

Zhang, S. and Zhand, X. 2020. The Relationship between Vocabulary Knowledge and L2 Reading/Listening Comprehension: A Meta-Analysis. *Language Teaching Research*, **26**(4), pp. 696-725.

3 The power of a single sentence

There is a notable emphasis on the teaching and learning of vocabulary, which is entirely justified – words serve as the foundational elements that give significance to what is being said or read. Certainly, many words are acquired incidentally, and their meanings are readily understood through identifiable objects, pictures or context. However, some words require explicit instruction, leading students to quickly recognise the importance of specific words and phrases. Furthermore, there is a justified focus on ensuring that students comprehend the texts they read and study during lessons. Teachers can achieve this by summarising the main ideas, providing bullet points outlining key events or presenting facts using visual aids like diagrams, photographs and graphic organisers.

Nevertheless, it is essential to consider how often we concentrate on individual sentences. How frequently do we teach students how to read a single sentence? How thorough are we in establishing the meanings and relationships between the words within a single sentence? How routinely do we introduce new and unfamiliar words and promptly proceed to full passages without offering the foundational step of 'dissecting' a sentence? Do we assume that students know and can write 'good' sentences across the curriculum or do we take the initiative to instruct them in various techniques of sentence and by doing so eliminate any reliance on chance? In the pursuit of comprehensive language comprehension, it is vital to address these questions and give due attention to the intricacies of individual sentences as a fundamental aspect of language learning.

Relationships within a single sentence

Analysing and studying **relationships between words within a single sentence** can be a highly effective strategy for training students in reading and comprehending complex sentences. Identifying the *subject + verb* in a sentence draws students' attention to the essential information in a complex statement. Subject is understood as the noun, pronoun or noun phrase that typically performs the action of the verb and typically is the topic or focus of the sentence. Sentences with multiple subjects may, specifically, pose difficulties for multilingual learners. Let's examine the following sentence used in a science lesson:

> The food we eat has to be broken down into other substances that our bodies can use.

For proficient language users and readers, this single-line sentence may not pose a significant challenge. However, students who are still developing proficiency in a second language may struggle to comprehend the overall meaning if they read each word in isolation. To alleviate this issue, teachers can provide guidance and modelling by introducing simple tasks such as identifying subjects and verbs. This approach facilitates a deeper understanding of sentence structure and enhances comprehension skills.

What is the subject of 'eat'? (Who or what performs the action of eating?)
What is the subject of 'has to be broken down'? (What 'has to be broken down'?)
What noun does 'that' refer to?

The subject of 'eat' is 'we'. 'We' is a pronoun that represents the person or people consuming the food. The subject of 'has to be broken down' is 'food'. 'Food' is the noun that is being acted upon (passive voice) in the sentence. The word 'that' refers to 'other substances. It serves as a relative pronoun connecting the dependent clause 'that our bodies can use' to the noun 'substances'. It indicates that the substances are thrones our bodies can utilise.

Since 'food' is the main subject in this sentence, the essential element carrying the meaning is the information that refers to it. The phrase 'we eat' provides additional information and is not crucial to the overall meaning of the statement.

> The food [we eat] has to be broken down into other substances that our bodies can use.

Alternatively, the sentence could be broken into two separate ones to ensure that the meaning is clear to students.

> The food has to be broken down into other substances.
> Our bodies can use these other substances.

Breaking long and complex sentences into simple and shorter sentences might be particularly beneficial to students who are new to English. It is important, though, that we provide opportunities for students to be exposed to, read, interact with, analyse and reflect on **the meaning and structures of complex sentences**. If students are to develop skills in understanding the relationships between words, phrases and clauses within sentences, they need a chance to practise. This practice will better equip them when reading complex texts independently.

Let's take a look at another example. This sentence comes from a history lesson:

> Firstly, widespread discontent among the Russian population due to economic inequality and social justice created a sense of frustration and anger.

56 The power of a single sentence

Confident readers and proficient language users are able to **break down sentences into meaningful parts**, focusing on the essential information. They can also identify additional, non-essential details within the sentence. Teaching students effective strategies for approaching such sentences can greatly impact their success in understanding longer passages. Identifying the subject in the sentence and the verb will allow students to focus on the core of the sentence and contribute to a better understanding of key information, rather than trying to process everything at once. Encouraging students to chunk the sentence, along with the visual in Figure 3.1, can be helpful.

The example in Figure 3.2 demonstrates how the graph might be completed. The darker boxes contain the essential information, while the lighter boxes provide additional details.

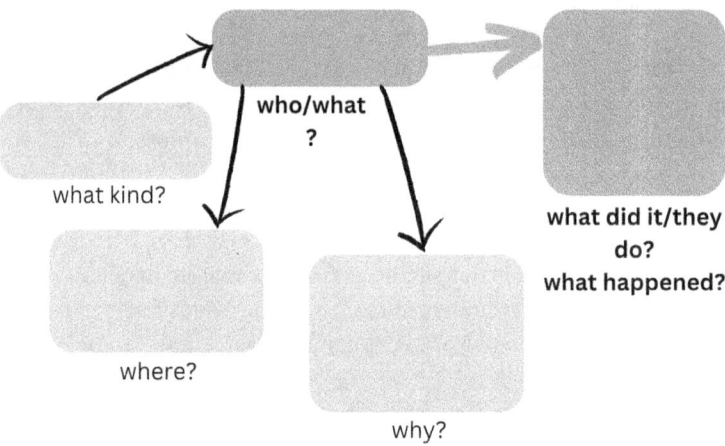

Figure 3.1 Chunking sentences into smaller units can enhance comprehension by breaking down complex information into more manageable, digestible segments, making it easier for students to grasp and process the content.

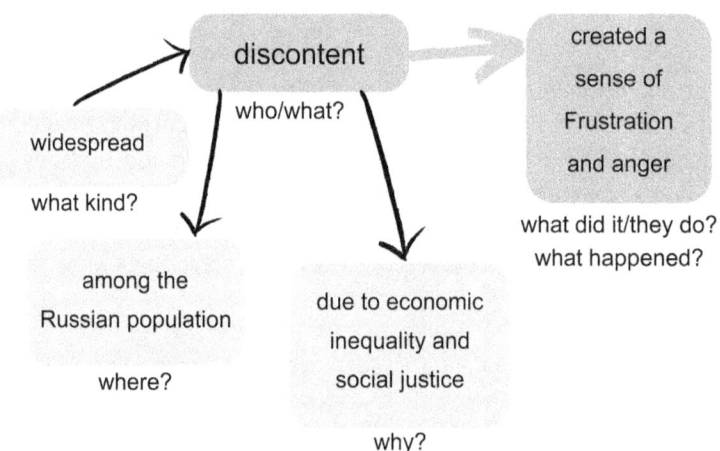

Figure 3.2 This process of chunking sentences can be initially modelled by the teacher, enabling students to subsequently practise it independently.

The power of a single sentence 57

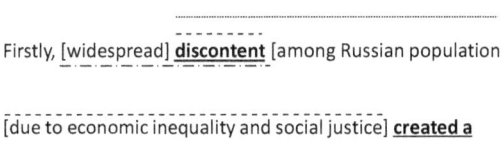

Figure 3.3 Students can learn how to systematically divide a sentence into distinct, digestible segments, aiding their comprehension.

With practice, students should become proficient at annotating sentences without relying on the need to draw diagrams. Identifying and labelling different parts of a sentence might be enough when focussing on the key messages, as shown in Figure 3.3.

Initially, the task of labelling and annotating sentences may be performed using a pen or a highlighter, enabling students to clearly discern and concentrate on essential segments and critical information. As learners become more adept and self-assured with the procedure, they can carry it out mentally while reading a text.

Speaking in full sentences

We do not always speak in full sentences, whether it is during casual conversations or more formal academic exchanges. **Natural speech** often consists of sentence fragments, pauses, interjections, reformulations, hesitations or false starts. The last one refers to a situation where a speaker begins saying something but then interrupts or changes their course before completing the sentence or thought. This can occur due to uncertainty or because the speaker wants to revise or correct what they are saying. It happens regardless of whether the speaker is monolingual or multilingual.

Let's examine an exchange between a teacher and a student that includes reformulation and revision of the answer, which is typical in spontaneous conversations.

> Teacher: Is Romeo portrayed as a violent character?
>
> Student: Yes, he is. Ummmm...I think...well, at the beginning of the play he isn't violent. Later, his attitude changes. He becomes more aggressive when Tybalt kills Mercutio.

Certainly, it is easy to imagine the following conversation below:

> Teacher: Is Romeo portrayed as a violent character?
>
> Student: Yes, he is.   or   No, he isn't.

The teacher could encourage or insist that the students' answers are based on the question and the words used in the question. The exchange might unfold as follows:

> Teacher: Is Romeo portrayed as a violent character?
>
> Student: Yes, Romeo is portrayed as a violent character.

All three examples are valid. Which one do you consider to be the most natural? As for accepting an answer from a student, I would choose the first one. The second response is not detailed at all, while the last one, with the exact use of the named words from the question, might sound slightly unnatural.

The aim is to develop students' knowledge and enhance their ability to effortlessly produce detailed responses using contextually appropriate words and phrases. Achieving this requires ample practice, which can be facilitated by asking students to reuse words and phrases from the question. While this may not reflect the way most people speak in everyday conversations, it proves highly beneficial for multilingual learners. Let's examine the two examples below:

> Teacher: What did Tsar Nicholas forbid?
>
> Student A: The formation of political parties.
> Student B: Tsar Nicholas forbade the formation of political parties.

Insisting on using full sentences has two-fold benefits: it **enhances message clarity and provides an opportunity for practice**. It is worth noting that the word 'forbade', used in the past tense (the second form of the verb 'forbid') in Student's B response, may not frequently be encountered in everyday conversations. If students are not exposed to and do not actively use such words in the spoken language, they are less likely to incorporate them into their written responses. Monolingual speakers, who are aware of the past tense of the verb 'forbid' through the use of full sentences, can provide valuable listening and noticing practice for other students. By establishing the answer as 'Tsar Nicholas forbade the formation of political parties', another student can be encouraged to expand on their ideas by repeating the full sentence and adding 'because' to provide more detailed information.

Speaking in full sentences enables students to hear a complete message instead of fragmented parts, allowing them to 'observe' how syntax changes. This practice directs students' attention towards grammatical patterns. For instance, questions in the past simple tense generally include 'did' followed by the first form of the verb, while answers require the second form of the verb. Moreover, practising answering in full sentences serves as a valuable exercise before writing, as students will likely be expected to compose extended written pieces at some point. Opting for words and phrases instead of well-constructed sentences may not be a viable option in such scenarios.

However, it is important to note that initially, students may heavily rely on the wording of the questions and use them verbatim in their answers. I do not believe it is necessary to enforce a strict rule about this. As students gain confidence and fluency, they will naturally want and should be encouraged to explore alternative ways of expressing their ideas, rather than strictly adhering to familiar patterns. While reusing question structures to form answers can be helpful, it may lead to formulaic or incomplete responses lacking in detail. Thus, it is crucial to foster an environment where students feel empowered to express themselves in a comprehensible manner, without always requiring full sentences.

Teaching sentence writing explicitly

The importance of focusing on and imparting **content (the 'what')** in mainstream lessons is beyond question. Lessons should strongly revolve around content, with students acquiring and deepening their knowledge of specific subjects. However, to assert that concentrating solely on knowledge and neglecting to explicitly teach or highlight **language (the 'how')** is sufficient would overlook the mutually co-existent nature of these two components.

I once observed a geography lesson in which students learned about the distinctive features of various environments. Each stage of the lesson was meticulously designed and built upon the previous one. There were ample opportunities for students to practise key vocabulary independently and in pairs, using both short phrases and full sentences. Photographs were effectively utilised and labelled and the teacher provided a model for the tasks, allowing students to engage in some independent work. This comprehensive approach culminated in the final and most substantial task of comparing and contrasting two habitats. Upon giving the instructions for the final task, I noticed several students freezing, their mini-whiteboards and pens at the ready. Some began writing, but many did not. It was noteworthy that most of these students were multilingual learners who required ongoing language support in mainstream lessons. This experience highlighted the crucial need to address language instruction alongside content in order to support the academic development of multilingual learners.

Explicitly instructing and demonstrating the **process of crafting responses** to questions can bring significant benefits at the sentence level. Once students have acquired and practised the foundational knowledge of the content, the emphasis should be placed on teaching them how to construct answers effectively. This aspect is of equal importance as it determines how subject knowledge is conveyed, depending on the common words used, such as 'describe', 'compare', 'contrast', 'evaluate', 'justify' and others. It is crucial to recognise that these words may require different interpretations based on the context of the lesson. For example, the term 'describe' will carry distinct implications in English and science classes. In an English lesson, it may prompt students to produce elaborate and emotionally or analytically charged sentences, whereas in a science lesson it may be as simple as creating a diagram to explain a complex system or experiment.

60 The power of a single sentence

In the context of a geography lesson focused on discussing different habitats, the teacher may adopt a **modelling technique** to exemplify the comparison and contrast of various features, using concise yet informative sentences. Employing the gradual release approach, students are granted increasing autonomy at each stage, enabling them to eventually formulate their own sentences. This method ensures meticulous attention to every aspect of sentence construction, encompassing the sentence's aim, appropriate punctuation and the positioning of conjunctions. Consequently, students are afforded ample opportunities to engage in purposeful and meaningful practice, thereby reinforcing both content comprehension and language proficiency at the same time.

In the example provided in Figure 3.4, students may receive either a partially pre-filled table or a blank one containing distinct features. Subsequently, they would be tasked with recalling relevant information about each feature, pertaining to a specific habitat.

The teacher could introduce the sentence structure for contrasting ideas by providing a model for the students to follow (Figure 3.5).

Feature	Desert habitat	Rainforest habitat
climate	dry, arid, minimal rainfall	high annual rainfall, humid
vegetation	sparse (mainly cacti and succulent plants)	diverse and dense
fauna	animals adapted to survive extreme conditions (camels, snakes, scorpions)	diverse range of species (birds, insects, mammals)
water sources	limited (oases, underground aquifers)	many (rivers, streams, rainfall)
biodiversity	low	high

Figure 3.4 Students may be asked to recall key information and organise it in a table, before writing full sentences.

Sentence 1.	In contrast, However, On the other hand,	sentence 2.

Figure 3.5 Modelling sentences is an effective technique and offers students easy steps to follow.

The power of a single sentence 61

The first sentence could be modelled by the teacher:

climate:

> *In the desert habitat, the climate is dry and arid with minimal rainfall. In contrast, in the rainforest habitat, the climate is humid with high levels of annual rainfall.*

The next sentence can be constructed collaboratively with the entire class or in pairs. The explicit scaffold remains readily available to support the process.

vegetation:

_____ ,

                      desert habitat   *However,*

                                                         In contrast,

                                                         On the other hand,

_____ .

                      rainforest habitat

The final step of the process involves enabling learners to write the sentences independently. Depending on the students' proficiency levels, certain scaffolding may still be provided or removed entirely.

fauna:

_____ . _____ ,

_____ .

Providing students with **exposure to diverse sentence structures** and ensuring plenty of opportunities for practice will enable them to produce clear, grammatically accurate sentences that are easily comprehensible. Through consistent practice over time, students will develop the ability to articulate the content of their lessons using a multitude of language functions effectively. For instance, the process can be modelled when one sentence is involved (Figure 3.6).

Sentence 1.	whereas while	sentence 2.

Figure 3.6 Using consistent patterns will allow for students' increased independence.

Statement1	differs from that contrasts with that	statement 2	because of _____ . due to _____ .

Figure 3.7 Modelling how to write sentences can employ a certain level of flexibility.

water sources:

> In the desert habitat the water sources are limited <u>while</u> in the rainforest there are many water sources,
>
>   statement 1   statement 2
>
> for example rivers, streams and rainfall.

Or see Figure 3.7.

biodiversity:

> Biodiversity in the desert habitat <u>differs from that</u> in the rainforest habitat **due to** its comparatively low levels.

The above strategy clearly demonstrates the significance of **integrating language instruction throughout all subjects within the curriculum**. While knowledge of two different habitats may not appear essential in a history or art lesson, the proficiency in using language structures to compare and contrast historical events or diverse pieces of artwork contributes to the continuous development of language skills. This approach also underscores the importance of equipping students with cross-curricular vocabulary. When the ability to contrast (or justify, explain, analyse, describe, etc.) ideas is necessary across various subjects, it exemplifies how language skills operate on a spiral trajectory. Rather than starting at a fixed point each time, language skills can be progressively built upon and refined irrespective of the topics studied.

Summary

Why?

The use and modelling of full sentences in speaking and writing:

- highlights the syntax and grammatical rules.
- provides multilingual students with clear and comprehensible examples of well-structured sentences.

- allows to internalise the patterns and conventions of the target language.
- lays the groundwork for more complex skills, such as paragraph and essay writing.
- creates equitable access to language learning.
- allows students to observe how ideas are organised and conveyed leading to improved communication in speaking and writing.

How?

1. decide on the types of sentences to be modelled (these could be based on the overarching aim of the lesson, for example, comparing and contrasting ideas) or grammatical structures (for example, the use of past tenses).
2. provide clear and explicit explanations of sentence structure (for example, subject, verb, object, use of punctuation).
3. use visual aids like charts, diagrams or graphic organisers to illustrate the various elements of a sentence and their relationships.
4. include appropriate scaffolding, such as sentence frames or starters. Gradually remove the support to allow independent practice.
5. live model the writing of sentences while narrating your choices.

Levels

A-E:

- sentence structure and complexity can be adjusted based on students' levels.
- writing can be completed independently or in pairs/groups.
- sentence stems or frames are provided to support learners in constructing their sentences.
- visuals (charts or graphs) are provided to aid comprehension.

References

Gibbons, P. 1993. *Learning to Learn in a Second Language*. Portsmouth: Heinemann.

Gibbons, P. 2015. *Scaffolding Language, Scaffolding Learning: Teaching Second Language Learners in Mainstream Classroom*. Portsmouth: Heinemann.

Grellet, F. 1981. *Developing Reading Skills*. Cambridge: Cambridge University Press.

Hochman, J. C. and Wexler, N. 2017. *The Writing Revolution: A Guide to Advancing Thinking through Writing in all Subjects and Grades*. San Francisco: Jossey-Bass.

4 Navigating the worlds of words
Reading skills and EAL learners

Reading, an indispensable skill in our information-driven world, is undeniably complex and multifaceted for both multilingual and monolingual learners. It extends far beyond the mere decoding of letters and words; it involves a delicate interplay of language acquisition, encompassing a vast vocabulary, grammatical and syntactical structures, often nuanced and idiosyncratic spelling rules, background knowledge and cultural references. Given the intricate and multilayered nature of reading, it becomes evident that many EAL learners possess both advantages and certain weaknesses in this skill (Joseph, 2022).

Linguists and researchers define reading skills as **a set of automatic abilities** and actions that proficient readers perform to comprehend a text (Adams, 1990; Richards, 2015; Thornbury, 2006). These essential reading skills encompass decoding (the ability to understand the letter-sound relationships for word pronunciation), linguistic comprehension (recognising and comprehending words, phrases and sentences within the text and understanding the grammatical and syntactical aspects of the language, including sentence structure), reading comprehension (the capacity to understand and make sense of the content and message conveyed in the text, going beyond linguistic comprehension by requiring the comprehension of main ideas, details, arguments and the overall purpose of the text) and fluency (pertaining to the rhythm, intonation, pace and expression in reading).

The ability to decode words and sentences is usually achieved relatively quickly by multilingual learners, as it is perceived as a comparatively simpler task. Additionally, many multilingual learners can often read in their first languages, and **Common Underlying Language Proficiency**, along with positive transfer, may play a contributing role. On the other hand, the process of learning and remembering new words in various contexts, building a schema of background knowledge and developing reading comprehension skills takes time (Joseph, 2022).

It is, therefore, crucial to ascertain the position of EAL students on their reading journey. The time students dedicate to the processes of decoding, understanding words or sentences and comprehending whole passages will vary based on their mastery of decoding skills, the extent of their familiar vocabulary, the content they read, their existing schema and the specific objectives associated with a given text (Watkins, 2017). Consequently, some students may greatly benefit from personalised and targeted support in phonics, grammar, sentence structure or vocabulary development. The development of reading skills should also be actively integrated into mainstream lessons by intentionally employing specific approaches and techniques while reading a text, aiming to facilitate a comprehensive understanding of written words (Richards, 2015).

Mainstream lessons offer an optimal environment for multilingual students to learn and practise reading. In these settings, students are **immersed in the target language**, providing them with exposure to diverse vocabulary within the context of their regular academic curriculum. This exposure to vocabulary, in authentic contexts is essential, as it allows students to understand the nuanced meanings and usages of words, phrases and idiomatic expressions – these are often taught explicitly to all students. Moreover, the texts used in mainstream lessons often mirror the kind of material students will encounter later in their academic lives and exams, making it a practical and relevant learning experience. In the process of engaging with these texts, students also learn new words incidentally, without the need for explicit vocabulary instruction, thereby expanding their language proficiency.

This chapter will place its primary focus on the exploration of effective reading strategies and tasks tailored not only to EAL learners but all within mainstream lessons. By understanding and implementing these strategies and tasks, EAL learners can make significant progress in their reading abilities, enabling them to engage more fully with their peers in mainstream lessons and attain greater academic success.

I have worked with many learners who were confident readers in their first languages but in the early stages of learning English. (Un)surprisingly, many of them were able to answer some comprehension-testing questions based on GCSE-level texts. They were able to do so not because the content was fully accessible and comprehensible, but because they were able to apply the same techniques and strategies when reading texts in their own languages. The students who had studied English as a foreign language abroad were also aware that the order in which the questions are written is usually the order in which the answers are presented in the text. When we ask students to read a text and answer a series of questions based on that particular text to check their understanding, we adopt a test-based approach. Students might be actually quite successful at completing the task (that is answering questions by locating a keyword from the question, finding it in the text and using the identified phrase or sentence surrounding the clue). Of course, this is a great start and a strategy of identifying keywords should be employed by learners. The task, however, is fully meaningful if learners can understand what they read rather than perform a mechanical action of copying chunks of text.

Additionally, the transfer of reading strategies, or the ability to use a variety of strategies that have been learnt in one context or language, and used to understand a text in a different situation, should be recognised, valued and regularly practised. If, for example, a student is skilled at using a previewing strategy of looking at the title, headings, illustrations in a science textbook, they will be able to do the same when reading a news article. Reading strategies are an important aspect of developing more independent and self-directed readers who can approach new texts with a degree of confidence and reflection on what is the most effective strategy for a particular text. The level of confidence might depend on the similarities and differences between the texts but also on the readers' metacognitive skills, and their ability to employ an array of the most appropriate strategies.

Graphic organisers for reading

The concept of graphic organisers has evolved over time, used and adapted by various organisations and groups of people. Visual representation to organise information started to be used more commonly in the 19th century when diagrams were utilised to classify and represent knowledge in the fields of science and mathematics. In education, graphic organisers are used as an instructional tool for reading comprehension and written expression. Their use across multiple subjects and disciplines is versatile and can serve many purposes. They help to **visualise information and make connections between ideas**. As they provide a structured format for representing information, they can be especially useful when complex ideas are discussed. Moreover, they allow learners to actively engage with the material, and that can increase the level of understanding and information retention.

While graphic organisers are instrumental in visually structuring information, concepts, thoughts and ideas when writing (as we will discuss later), they also serve to emphasise and bring to the forefront the specific language requirements necessary to accomplish a given task. For instance, a Venn diagram incorporates the language functions of comparison and contrast, while flow charts depict processes and sequences of events, underscoring the need for language that describes the order of events or a series of actions. Hence, it can be advantageous to place emphasis on cohesive devices, such as linkers (e.g., 'first', 'then', 'next', 'the penultimate step', etc.), or the use of the present tense to describe a process. For instance, when describing the process of evaporation, employing the present simple tense can be quite effective, as in 'it occurs' and 'the water changes into a gaseous state', among others.

A **sociogram**, a type of graphic organiser, is a visual representation of the relationships between groups or characters in a group. Drawing a sociogram could be exploited as a reading strategy which involves a non-linguistic or very succinct response to a text. The students have to actively engage with the text and depict the relationships between the characters. The activity could start with students identifying and underlining or highlighting the names of all the characters described (this allows the learners to practise scanning skills), categorising protagonists according to a particular character trait, affiliation to a certain group or originating from a given place or family ties. The students present the information in the form of a diagram showing their understanding of the relationships between the characters. The task could be easily scaffolded depending on the students' levels of language by, for example, providing a ready-to-be-filled template, naming the type of relationship between the key figures, adding extra details on each person, etc.

The examples below show how students can actively engage with reading curriculum-related texts focusing on deepening their understanding of the relationships between the main characters in Shakespeare's *Romeo and Juliet*. The activity is also a perfect opportunity to highlight some language points which could be challenging to some multilingual learners, for example the use of possessive 's: this grammatical construction indicates ownership or possession of something. In English the possessive 's is typically added to the end of a noun or a name. It is not a contracted form of 'is' as it is the case in the sentence 'Romeo's an impulsive young man'. Another point which might be discussed is the use of the present simple tense to summarise the events and relationships between the main protagonists. Once the students have completed the sociogram and created a web of associations and bonds, they could be asked to present them orally and in writing, relying only on the visual representation.

> The main characters are Romeo and Juliet and their respective families, the Montagues and the Capulets. Romeo is a Montague and Juliet is a Capulet. The two families are sworn enemies and are engaged in a long-standing feud. Despite this, Romeo and Juliet fall in love at first sight and secretly marry. Other important characters in the play include Friar Laurence, a well-respected and wise friar who assists Romeo and Juliet in their relationship; Mercutio, Romeo's best friend; and Tybalt, Juliet's hot-headed cousin who is fiercely loyal to the Capulet family. Paris is a young nobleman and kinsman of the Prince of Verona who is seeking to marry Juliet, even though she does not love him. He is initially courteous and respectful towards Juliet, but she is already in love with Romeo and rejects Paris's advances.

The strategy of mapping the relationships between the characters in novels, plays and poems studied in English lessons can be used in other subjects. In history, for example, the students can visually represent the dynamics in relationships between the countries

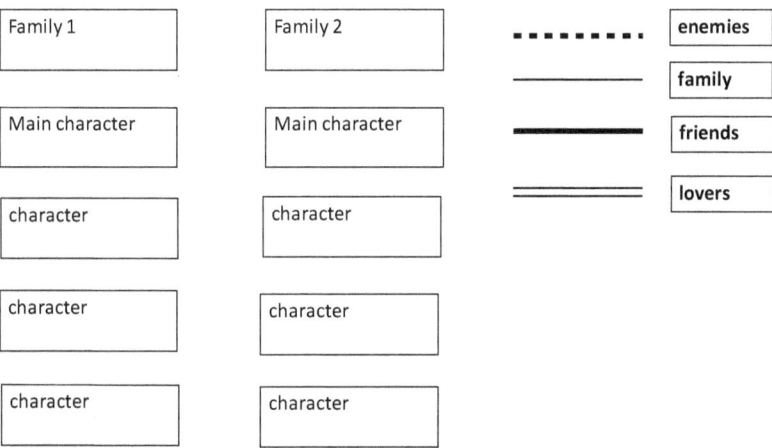

Figure 4.1 Graphic organisers can prove highly effective in facilitating comprehension.

at a given time. The example below depicts the complex map of intertwined connections between the countries before and during World War II.

> Germany, Italy and Japan formed the Axis Powers and were enemies of the Allied Powers, which included countries such as the United States, Britain, France, the Soviet Union and China. The Axis Powers sought to expand their territories and influence, while the Allied Powers aimed to stop them and protect their own interests. The relationships between countries during World War II were often complex and constantly shifting. For example, the Soviet Union initially signed a non-aggression pact with Germany in 1939 but later became an ally of the Allied Powers after Germany invaded the Soviet Union in 1941.
>
> Similarly, the United States initially remained neutral in the war but provided aid to the Allied Powers through the Lend-Lease Act. After Japan attacked Pearl Harbour in 1941 the United States officially entered the war and became a key ally of the Allied Powers.

The students engage with a complex and academic text. Whilst they gain or review their knowledge, they read a passage written in a formal register and objective tone; it is rigorous and challenging, both in terms of the content and the language. The learners, however, are not simply asked to read the text and answer the comprehension checking questions. They are required to reflect the complexity of connections between the states by annotating a diagram, describing the situation orally and finally writing their responses down. At every single stage of this task, the students have a chance to rehearse their responses, improving and crafting them in terms of grammar, use of academic lexis and gaining more confidence with pronunciation, sentence structure and cohesion of their extended answers.

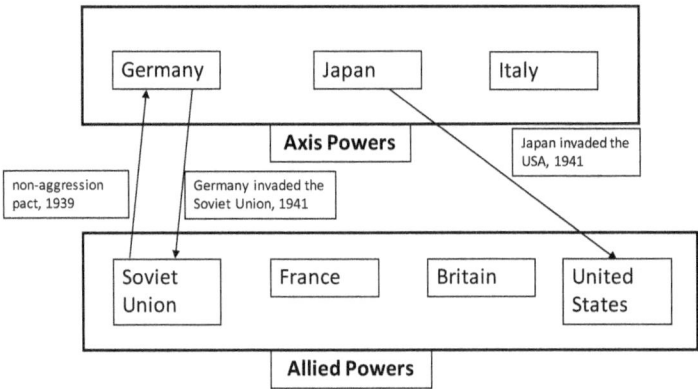

Figure 4.2 Teachers can effectively demonstrate the thinking process behind completing a graphic organiser, providing students with a valuable model.

Another example comes from a Religious Studies lesson. The following brief passage portrays intricate relationships amongst the predecessors of Jesus. Furthermore, the text lacks a clear chronological arrangement of events so the exploration of their sequence might form part of the lesson. Instead of relying on interrogative prompts such as 'when', 'who' or 'where', it may prove more effective to methodically map the sequence of events and emphasise the interconnected network of relationships among the individuals and groups mentioned in the text.

> Where was Jesus from?
>
> After being liberated from slavery, the Jews (also known as the 'Israelites') were led by Moses on a journey between Egypt and Canaan. Eventually, they returned to the 'Promised Land', which was the region of Canaan where Abraham, Isaac and Jacob had previously resided.
>
> Many years later, David, a descendant of Jacob's son Judah, ascended to the throne as the King of Judea around 885 BCE. He captured Jerusalem and established it as the capital of Israel. Nearly 1,000 years following David's reign, Jesus Christ was born in Roman-controlled Judea.
>
> Jesus was born in Bethlehem, located in Judea. His mother Mary, a virgin, was engaged to Joseph, a descendant of King David. The name Jesus originates from the Hebrew name 'Joshua', which means 'he who saves', and 'Christ' is derived from the Hebrew term 'mashiach', signifying 'messiah'. Christians firmly believe that Jesus is the chosen saviour of humanity, whereas Jews maintain the belief that the messiah is yet to come.

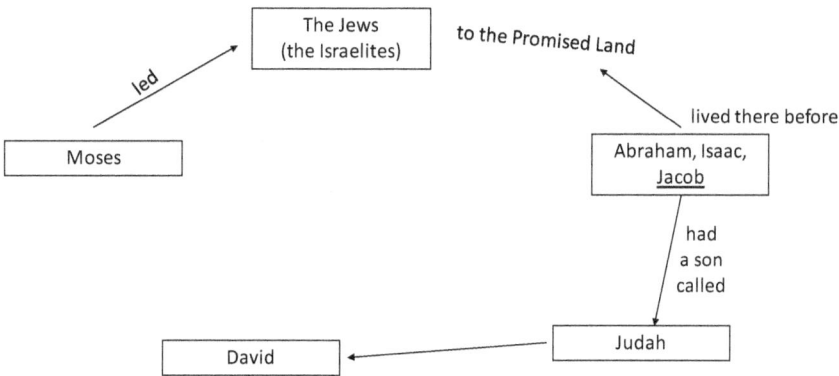

Figure 4.3 In addition to illustrating the relationships between key figures, graphic organisers in reading can also depict the sequence of events.

70 Navigating the worlds of words

 Circle the names of people or groups mentioned in the text.

 Describe the connections and links between them.

To further reinforce the students' understanding of the sequence of events, they could complete another task that will require referring back to the text. To confirm the order of events, students have to focus on the key, pertinent points and finish the sentences below using one of the following words:

during   after   before   since   while

1. _____ being freed from slavery, the Jews were led by Moses on a journey between Egypt and Canaan.
2. They came back to the 'Promised Land' where Abraham, Isaac and Jacob lived _____.
3. _____ in power, many years later, David captured Jerusalem and established it as the capital of Israel.
4. Jesus Christ was born _____ the times when the Romans controlled Judea.
5. _____ his birth in Bethlehem, Jesus has been regarded as a saviour of humanity.

Summary

Why?

Graphic organisers:

- enhance reading, speaking, listening and writing skills.
- facilitate students' comprehension of textual content.
- are extremely versatile and can be used for a variety of tasks across the curriculum.

How?

1. students or the teacher begin by reading a text that describes the relationships between main characters, countries, places, etc.
2. either individually, in pairs or small groups, students reread the text and create a diagram to illustrate the relationships between the key parties. To aid in this process, a template and a legend (which may include pictures) can be provided.

3. students then proceed to describe the diagram they have created.
4. finally, either individually or collaboratively, students write down the description of the diagram, trying to recreate the original text.

Levels

A-E:

- the texts can be adapted to suit students' proficiency levels.
- use a partially completed diagram.
- students complete the diagram either independently, in pairs or small groups.

Cohesion: what keeps the text together?

Graphic organisers are valuable tools for enhancing our understanding of how events and characters in a story or text are connected. These visual aids can effectively highlight the **relationships within the narrative**. Additionally, paying attention to cohesive devices within the text can further assist in tracking these connections, ultimately improving comprehension. When we use graphic organisers, we create visual representations of the story's structure, which might include diagrams, flowcharts or concept maps. These organisers help us see how events unfold and how characters interact. They provide a visual roadmap, making it easier to grasp the sequence of events and the roles characters play in the narrative.

Cohesion in reading, on the other hand, refers to the way that different **elements within a text are connected to one another** to create a unified and coherent piece of writing (Thornbury, 1997). It is an important aspect of comprehension and understanding when it comes to reading. Cohesion is achieved through various linguistic devices and strategies that help guide readers through the text, making the relationships between sentences and paragraphs clear.

Let's take a look at these two sentences describing Dracula.

> *Dracula's* **long moustache** *and* **bushy eyebrows** made him look sinister. **Not only** his **facial hair but also** his black clothes were disturbing.

In the sentence, cohesion is achieved through coordination. The coordinating conjunction 'and' is used to connect the two elements, 'Dracula's long moustache' and 'bushy eyebrows'. This conjunction signals that these two elements are related and should be considered together in terms of their effect on Dracula's appearance. In the second sentence, there is a use of correlative conjunctions 'not only...but also', which serves to emphasise the relationship between the two elements, 'his facial hair' and 'his black clothes'. The phrase 'not only...but also' creates a parallel structure and highlights that both aspects of Dracula's appearance contribute to his sinister and disturbing demeanour. The phrase 'facial hair' refers back to the description in the first sentence. By using 'facial hair', the second sentence maintains cohesion by drawing a direct connection between Dracula's moustache and eyebrows and the subsequent reference to his disturbing black clothes. Explaining these connections whilst a text is read in class, will help students understand the logical flow of passages. This might also impact students writing in a positive way as they will focus their attention on establishing explicit and well-structured relationships between ideas (Gibbons, 1993, 2015; Grellet, 1981).

Key elements of cohesion in reading include:

- **pronouns:** the use of pronouns (e.g., he, she, it, they) to refer back to previously mentioned nouns. Pronouns help maintain continuity and reduce redundancy in a text.
- **reference:** referring to specific elements within the text, such as people, objects or concepts, using words or phrases. This ensures that readers can track the relationships between different parts of the text.
- **conjunctions:** the use of words like 'and', 'but', 'because' and others to connect ideas and indicate the logical relationships between sentences and clauses.
- **lexical cohesion:** This involves using words with related meanings or using repetition of keywords to link sentences or ideas. It can include synonyms, antonyms or words that are in some way semantically related.
- **ellipsis:** the omission of words or phrases that can be easily inferred from the context. Ellipsis helps to avoid unnecessary repetition and keeps the text concise.
- **substitution:** replacing a word or phrase with a substitute word (often a pronoun) to maintain clarity and coherence.
- **parallelism:** structuring sentences or phrases in a parallel manner, making it easier for the reader to follow the logic of the text.

Teaching cohesion in reading can be accomplished by focusing on the use of **transitional words and phrases to connect ideas within a text**. Encouraging students to identify and analyse pronouns, references and other cohesive devices helps them understand how sentences and paragraphs relate to one another. Guided discussions and practice activities that emphasise these elements can improve students' comprehension of how texts maintain logical flow and coherence.

Summary

Why?

Cohesive devices:

- help students understand and follow the flow of a text.
- enhance clarity, making written and spoken language more organised and understandable.
- facilitate conveying ideas logically and coherently.
- help students write cohesive and well-structured answers.

How?

1. explain the concept of cohesive devices and their role in connecting ideas within a text. Emphasise their importance in making language coherent and comprehensible.
2. provide examples of cohesive devices, including pronouns, conjunctions, transitional phrases and referencing techniques. Encourage students to identify them in texts and practise spotting them in sentences and paragraphs.
3. analyse written and spoken texts with students, highlighting how cohesive devices are used by authors and speakers to create cohesion and coherence.
4. encourage students to use cohesive devices in their own writing and speaking. Assign writing tasks that require the application of these devices. Provide feedback to help students refine their usage.
5. teach how different genres (e.g., narratives, essays, reports) may require specific cohesive devices. Explain how these devices contribute to the conventions of each genre.
6. incorporate cohesive device evaluation during the revision and editing process. Teach students to self-edit for cohesion and coherence.

Levels

A-E:

- the number and complexity of the devices introduced to students.
- the complexity of the texts they are working with might be adjusted.

A few words about pictures

Visual aids, such as pictures, diagrams, videos or tangible objects, serve as invaluable tools in mainstream lessons for EAL learners. These visual elements play a pivotal role in helping students establish meaning by providing a concrete and immediate connection between the language they are learning and the concepts or ideas they need to comprehend. **Visuals often transcend language barriers**, enabling EAL learners to grasp the content more readily particularly if they are used to name a concrete item without nuanced or multiple meanings. They offer a universal means of communication making complex topics more accessible. Whether it is a vivid image illustrating a new vocabulary word, a diagram clarifying a scientific concept or a video bringing historical events to life, these visual aids enhance the learning experience, fostering deeper understanding and engagement among EAL students in mainstream classrooms.

Many authentic texts indeed use visual aids, such as graphs, pictures, tables or pictures which either directly deliver information or add to the meaning of a text they accompany. Visual literacy, or the ability to interpret visuals, is crucial in this case to understanding and remembering a text (Rakes, Rakes and Smith, 1995). Visual aids not only aid comprehension and introduce plenty of background information (Thornbury, 2006) but also might significantly contribute to the readers' engagement and interest in what is being read (Harmer, 1998).

74 *Navigating the worlds of words*

The activity below uses several pictures as a strategic scaffold and is centred around a short text. By repeatedly focusing on specific key words within the text, the activity aims to 'zoom in' on language, ensuring that these linguistic components are thoroughly understood and practised. It is **a deliberate and intensive approach** that hones in on the vocabulary, providing students with ample opportunities to become familiar with and proficient in using these key words. The consistent use of pictures alongside the text is a strategic choice, as it initially establishes the meaning through visual cues, making the linguistic elements more accessible to learners.

1. Read the text below.

   In the play, Brutus joins **a conspiracy** led by Cassius to **assassinate** Julius Caesar, to **prevent** him from becoming **a tyrant**. Caesar's right-hand man Antony stirs up **hostility** against the conspirators and Rome becomes embroiled in a dramatic **civil war**.

2. What do the highlighted words mean? Match the pictures with the words. (Figure 4.4.)

Figure 4.4 Using visuals aids supports multilingual learners in establishing and reinforcing the meaning of new words.

3. Read the text again. Match the words and the definitions.

*In the play, Brutus joins **a conspiracy** led by Cassius to **assassinate** Julius Caesar, to **prevent** him from becoming **a tyrant**. Caesar's right-hand man Antony stirs up **hostility** against the conspirators and Rome becomes embroiled in a dramatic **civil war**.*

Word	definition
1. a conspiracy	to murder someone as a political act _____
2. (to) assassinate	a war between different groups of people who live in the same country _____
3. (to) prevent	someone who helps and supports you in your work _____
4. a tyrant	to become deeply involved in something _____
5. a right-hand man	to stop something, to ensure that something does not happen _____
6. embroiled in	the secret planning by a group of people to do something illegal _____
7. civil war	someone who treats others in a cruel and unfair way _____
8. hostility	unfriendly, aggressive behaviour towards people and their ideas _____

4. Read the text using words in place of the pictures. Then write down the missing words. (Figure 4.5.)

In the play, Brutus joins _____ led by Cassius to _____ Julius Caesar, to _____ him from becoming _____ . Caesar's right-hand man Antony stirs up _____ against the conspirators and Rome becomes embroiled in a dramatic _____ .

In the play, Brutus joins [picture] led by Cassius to [picture] Julius Caesar, to [picture] him from becoming [picture] .Caesar's right-hand man Antony stirs up [picture] against the conspirators and Rome becomes embroiled in a dramatic [picture] .

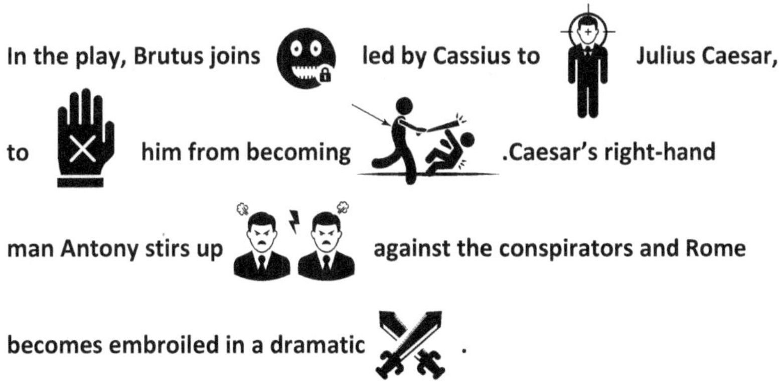

Figure 4.5 Consistent use of the same pictures supports multilingual learners in memorising the words more effectively.

5. Read and then write the text by replacing the highlighted phrases with the words you have practised.

   *In the play, Brutus joins a **secret planning group** led by Cassius to **kill** Julius Caesar **for political reasons**, to **stop** him from becoming a **cruel and unfair ruler**. Caesar's **helper and supporter** Antony stirs up **aggressive behaviour** against **the people plotting against Julius Caesar** and Rome becomes **involved** in a dramatic **conflict between people who live in the same country**.*

While this activity is particularly concentrated, it serves a crucial purpose in reinforcing language skills. It is important to note that not all activities need to be or should be as intensive, as this approach may vary depending on the learning aims. However, it effectively builds a strong foundation of linguistic comprehension and usage for EAL learners.

Summary

Why?

Visuals:

- provide a visual reference that enhances comprehension and makes abstract concepts more tangible.
- make it easier for EAL students to understand and communicate ideas without relying solely on their developing language skills.
- can make learning more accessible, promoting a positive attitude towards language acquisition.

How?

1. choose pictures that are contextually relevant ensuring they support understanding and enhance comprehension.
2. select clear, high-quality images that are easily interpretable.
3. connect pictures with relevant vocabulary, aiding word acquisition.
4. be aware of cultural nuances and avoid images that may be culturally insensitive or unfamiliar to EAL learners.
5. create exercises using pictures to engage students actively in articulating the content of lessons.
6. ensure that visuals are inclusive and representative of a diverse range of backgrounds and experiences.

Levels

A–C:

- pictures are particularly useful for students at A–C levels when new vocabulary is introduced.
- the use of visuals might also be beneficial for more proficient users, supporting the understanding of specific subject vocabulary or more abstract words.

References

Adams, M. J. 1990. *Beginning to Read: Thinking and Learning about Print*. Cambridge: MIT Press.

Gibbons, P. 1993. *Learning to Learn in a Second Language*. Portsmouth: Heinemann.

Gibbons, P. 2015. *Scaffolding Language, Scaffolding Learning: Teaching Second Language Learners in Mainstream Classroom*. Portsmouth: Heinemann.

Grellet, F. 1981. *Developing Reading Skills*. Cambridge: Cambridge University Press.

Harmer, J. 1998. *How to Teach English. The Introduction to the Practice of English Language Teaching*. Harlow: Pearson Education Limited.

Joseph, H. 2022. Reading for EAL Learners. In H. Chalmers, ed. *The ResearchED Guide to English as an Additional Language. An Evidence-Informed Guide for Teachers*. Woodbridge: John Catt, pp. 129-139.

Rakes, G., Rakes, T. and Smith, T. 1995. Using Visuals to Enhance Secondary Students' Understanding Comprehension of Expository Texts. *Journal of Adolescent & Adult Literacy*, **39**(1), pp. 46-54.

Richards, J. C. 2015. *Key Issues in Language Teaching*. Cambridge: Cambridge University Press.

Thornbury, S. 1997. *About Language. Tasks for Teachers of English*. Cambridge: Cambridge University Press.

Thornbury, S. 2006. *An A-Z of ELT. A Dictionary of Terms and Concepts*. Oxford: Macmillan Education.

Watkins, P. 2017. *Teaching and Developing Reading Skills*. Cambridge: Cambridge University Press.

5 Striking the balance
Simplification vs easification for EAL learners

Teachers often have an inclination to simplify language structures and avoid certain grammatical patterns when trying to make texts simpler, and therefore, more accessible to students. Modifying language can be an effective strategy, particularly for students in the early stages of learning English. It might also prove helpful, when used judiciously, to students at higher levels, particularly when introducing new and complex contexts. It is, however, neither possible nor desirable to replace and eliminate academic vocabulary and complex grammatical structures from our lessons. Moreover, it would be detrimental to students if they were shielded from challenging texts or seldom provided opportunities to engage with highly complex subject-specific reading and writing. Restricting students from encountering difficult texts or limiting their exposure to complex language would, eventually, hinder their academic growth and preparedness.

At the same time, it would be unrealistic to expect all multilingual learners, who are at different proficiency levels, to understand every word, phrase or grammatical structure used in mainstream lessons without any adjustment or modification. According to Stephen Krashen, a prominent linguist and educational researcher in the field of second language acquisition who popularised the notion of **comprehensible input**, language learners need to be exposed to input (language in any form) that is slightly beyond their current level of proficiency in order to progress and acquire new language skills. Krashen refers to this concept as '+1'. The '+1' represents comprehensible input in language learning: language structures that are just slightly more complex than what students are already familiar with. This challenges learners to reach a little beyond their comfort zone and encourages the gradual expansion of their language skills (Krashen, 1982).

If the input (written language used in materials and resources, verbal explanations) is too challenging, it might lead to students' frustration, lower their confidence, cause a lack of engagement and result in students 'switching off' during lessons. The notion of '+1' emphasises the importance of providing challenging but accessible input to language learners. The issue, of course, lies in the diversity of students in one given class. What is perfectly attainable for a multilingual student who has been attending a school where English is used as a language of instruction for the last three years might be currently out of reach for a learner who is a new arrival and a beginner in English.

While adapting original texts and resources, or even modifying them to facilitate access to the mainstream curriculum for multilingual learners, is justified and occasionally necessary, it is challenging to envision the creation of multiple, tiered and differentiated versions of a given task as a sustainable and highly effective long-term solution. It is doubtful that such an approach aligns with the interests of both teachers and students.

One might argue that grouping students based on their English language proficiency levels and providing them with appropriate resources could prove beneficial and responsive in light of the '+1' hypothesis. Such a personalised approach may be convincing in certain situations. Nevertheless, it is crucial to ensure that our environment remains inclusive rather than inadvertently exclusive. Given that **language development is a dynamic process** intertwined with content, especially in subject-based classrooms, it becomes imperative to closely monitor the levels of challenge faced by our students. Instead of replacing or simplifying the content, a more desirable approach involves employing scaffolding techniques and modifying resources to support the students effectively. This way, multilingual learners can engage with the subject matter at an appropriate level while continuing to develop their language skills in tandem.

What's the difference?

Simplification and easification are two potential pedagogical approaches that can be employed to expose multilingual learners to complex, content-based texts (Bhatia, 1983). The former involves **modifying the original text** through lexical substitutions or simplified syntax, while the latter uses **various easification devices** (e.g. illustrations, diagrams, questions) without altering the original version. Both approaches can be implemented in the classroom, with certain features requiring proactive steps and adjustments to the resources before a lesson, while others can be employed during an activity with the teacher modelling the reading process, chunking the text and sentences and asking leading questions as the text is read aloud.

It is important to emphasise that simplification and easification, although seemingly similar on the surface, exhibit distinct differences. In the case of simplification, it operates on a continuum. As mentioned earlier, simplification can be justified in certain instances. For example, when we are confident in our assessment of a student's English language proficiency levels and subject knowledge which may indicate that the text will surpass the learner's capabilities. However, as teachers, we must exercise caution to ensure that the simplified version provided remains true to the essence of the original content and textual features rather than presenting a mere simplistic account (Widdowson, 1978). The first approach, with some adjustments and modifications, preserves the essential textual characteristics of a specific genre or writing type. On the other hand, the second approach may often result in content-reduced materials that avoid nuanced aspects. This inadvertently risks compromising the ambitions and rigour of the curriculum.

Non-fiction texts

Let's examine how a range of texts can be simplified and easified to enhance accessibility for multilingual learners. Firstly, we will analyse a text used in a science lesson and investigate the various stages and levels of simplification and easification that can render it comprehensible to multilingual learners.

> The respiratory system
>
> The process of respiration begins when we inhale through our nose and mouth. Both these entry points filter and warm the incoming air before it travels further into the respiratory system. The air then moves down the trachea, a tube-like structure. The trachea allows air to pass through and prevents it from collapsing. The trachea divides into two bronchial tubes, one for each lung. These tubes further brand out into smaller and narrower airways called bronchioles, resembling a tree's pattern. The bronchioles lead to the lungs, which are two large organs located in the chest. Within the lungs, the bronchioles end in small, balloon-like structures called alveoli. During inhalation, oxygen-rich air enters the alveoli and oxygen molecules diffuse through the thin wall of the alveoli. At the same time, carbon dioxide moves from the bloodstream into the alveoli and is expelled during exhalation.

The simplification of a text can be accomplished by dividing lengthy and complex sentences into simpler and shorter ones. Likewise, certain words and phrases can be substituted with more familiar or commonly used ones in everyday language, facilitating better understanding for learners. However, it is crucial to retain subject-specific terminology without alteration or substitution, as doing so could impede students from acquiring essential knowledge and expressing key concepts in an academically appropriate manner.

Original sentence:

> The process of respiration begins when we inhale through our nose and mouth.

Simplified sentence:

> Respiration, or breathing, starts when we breathe in air through our nose and mouth.

Original sentence:

> Both these entry points filter and warm the incoming air before it travels further into the respiratory system.

Simplified sentence:

> Both our nose and mouth filter and warm the air we breathe in. Next, the air moves further into the respiratory system.

Striking the balance 81

The examples provided above maintain certain academic rigour and effectively convey essential knowledge necessary for the study of the respiratory system. It is crucial to carefully monitor students' language development to ensure that multilingual learners receive appropriate support (scaffolding) in accessing complex texts, rather than offering simple alternatives. By exposing students to academically challenging resources and providing them with strategies to comprehend such materials, we can systematically enhance their vocabulary and syntax skills.

Otherwise, some learners may reach a plateau in their language acquisition or resort to avoiding certain grammatical structures or phrases. **Avoidance**, a phenomenon where learners consciously or subconsciously avoid using specific aspects of the target language, may stem from a lack of confidence in using more complex yet less familiar and practised language patterns. As a result, they may prefer to use language that is familiar and comfortable to them. The sentences they construct might be grammatically and lexically correct, but they tend to follow the same patterns or rely on memorised expressions.

Easification, also referred to as **text engineering** (Billings and Walqui, n.d.), does not entail the extensive alterations that simplification involves. Instead, the original materials are retained, with the vocabulary and syntax remaining unchanged. Enhanced accessibility and ease of understanding are achieved through various other means. The following example illustrates how the original texts remain intact while incorporating certain modifications in its presentation, such as text chunking and numbering, colour coding, illustrations and glossaries in the form of a synonym provided in brackets.

The respiratory system

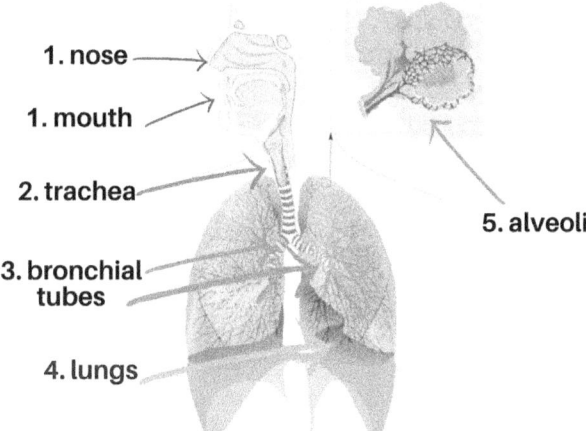

Figure 5.1 Labelling and colour-coding diagrams and pictures contributes to creating meaningful input.

1. **Nose and mouth**
    The process of respiration begins *(starts)* when we inhale through our **nose and mouth**. Both these entry points *(nose and mouth)* filter and warm the incoming air before it travels further into the respiratory system.
2. **Trachea**
    The air then moves down the **trachea**, a tube-like structure. The trachea allows air to pass through and prevents *(stops)* it from collapsing *(falling in)*.
3. **Bronchial tubes**
    The trachea divides into two **bronchial tubes**, one for each lung. These tubes further brand out *(divide)* into smaller and narrower airways called bronchioles, resembling *(looking like)* a tree's pattern.
4. **Lungs**
    The bronchioles lead to the **lungs**, which are two large organs located in the chest.
5. **Alveoli**
    Within the lungs, the bronchioles end in small, balloon-like structures called **alveoli**.
6. **Gas exchange**
    During inhalation, oxygen-rich air enters the alveoli and oxygen molecules diffuse through the thin wall of the alveoli. At the same time, carbon dioxide moves from the bloodstream into the alveoli and is expelled during exhalation.

The text can be presented to the students and the teacher will serve as a model, demonstrating the correct pronunciation of key words, appropriate use of punctuation and identifying the various elements and roles of the respiratory system. Students may be grouped in pairs or small groups to replicate the activity allowing them to practise the skills demonstrated by the teacher and improve their comprehension and confidence in using subject-specific and fundamental vocabulary.

To further ensure active engagement with the text and effective processing of new knowledge, as well as using lexical and grammatical structures for describing the respiratory system, guided activities can be provided. For instance, students could read the text and complete a diagram representing the respiratory system. Then, using only the graphic representation, they can describe it in pairs. This approach aims to enhance students' understanding of the respiratory system through interactive and participatory activities, enabling them to assimilate the language and knowledge effectively.

Arguably, one of the most challenging reading tasks lies in the comprehension of longer passages, chapters and complete novels and plays. In order to achieve success in English lessons at the secondary school level, students must possess the ability to narrate the general plot of a story, describe the main protagonists and their relationships, analyse the cultural and historical context and articulate their opinions on a given text. These skills are closely linked to the understanding of language at both **the semantic level** (comprehending the meaning of words and sentences) and **the syntactic level** (grasping the grammar and structure of sentences). For multilingual learners, mastering these foundational skills

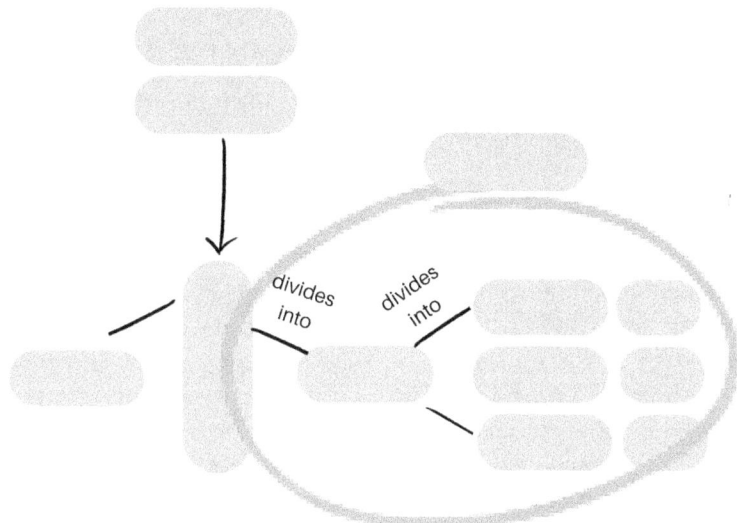

Figure 5.2 Graphic organisers assist students in breaking down longer texts into manageable sections while preserving the integrity of the ideas and writing style.

often serves as a prelude to the art of rhetoric, where students engage in deeper analysis of dialogues and characters, establish connections and analogies with other literary works and explore the perspective of different authors.

Alternative versions of non-fiction texts

Certain modifications can be applied to non-fiction texts to **enhance accessibility and comprehensibility**. These alterations might affect the wording to a certain degree but more importantly the presentation format (Bhatia, 1983; Bhatia, 1993). The form and structure of a text often play a pivotal role in defining its genre and subgenre; for example, recipes, job application emails or blog entries. When making such modifications, careful consideration should be given to the potential impact on the text's structure, particularly if learners are expected to produce similar texts. However, if the primary focus is on understanding the conveyed message, using alternative formats to prose becomes a viable option. This approach is particularly effective for non-sequential texts and allows readers to concentrate on small units of information at a time, presented through diagrams, flow charts or tables. Consequently, students gain access to the same information with some changes to the language used. The alternative version of the same text could be read and studied before or alongside the main text so that learners are still exposed to the language appropriate for a particular text.

The provided example comes from a science lesson, centres around the subject of genetics and the diversities in eye colour. The original text is presented in prose format.

There are three main eye colours that scientists have identified: brown, blue and green. Each gene has two versions, called alleles. Let's use the letters B and b to represent these alleles. The B allele is associated with brown eye colour and the b allele is associated with blue eye colour.

These are the possible combinations of these alleles and their probabilities:

- BB (two brown alleles): if both parents have brown eyes and each carries the BB genotype, then there is a 100% chance of inheriting a B allele from each parent. This means a child will have brown eyes.
- Bb (one brown allele and one blue allele): if one parent has brown eyes (Bb) and the other has blue eyes (bb), a child has a 50% chance of inheriting the B allele from the brown-eye parents and a 50% chance of inheriting the b allele from the blue-eyes parent. This means you have a 50% chance of having brown eyes and a 50% chance of having blue eyes.
- bb (two blue alleles): if both of the parents have blue eyes and each carries the bb genotype, the child has a 100% chance of inheriting a b allele from each parent. This means the child will have blue eyes.

Green eye colour is a result of more complex genetic interactions. The above probabilities provide a general idea; the actual outcome for any individual can vary.

Figure 5.3 and Figure 5.4 incorporate visual depictions that highlight the interrelationships and the varying probabilities associated with having distinct eye colours. In the first approach, the textual content is transformed into a diagram employing visual elements such as images and directional arrows. This facilitates an intentional focus on the underlying concepts, accommodating students whose linguistic proficiency may presently not align with the complexity of the original text. Following the teacher's explanation and students' scrutiny of the diagram, and establishing a firm grasp of the concept, attention may subsequently shift to the textual explanation, which can be placed adjacent to the diagram.

An alternative option involves segmenting the sentences into discrete units of information, subsequently ordering them in a sequential structure. Importantly, the linguistic content remains unaltered, yet its presentation is tailored to enhance students' comprehension.

An additional example is rooted in the discourse used within a history lesson. While minimal alterations to the language are evident when contrasted with the original text, the suggested adaptation of the text serves to empower students in discerning pivotal pieces of information categorised as positive and negative and further subdivided into social, economic and political dimensions. The layout of the text offers learners an organisational scaffold, enabling them to establish a framework into which they can seamlessly incorporate additional nuanced information without becoming unduly preoccupied with the specific relations underpinning these categories.

Striking the balance 85

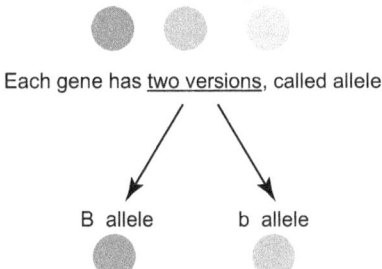

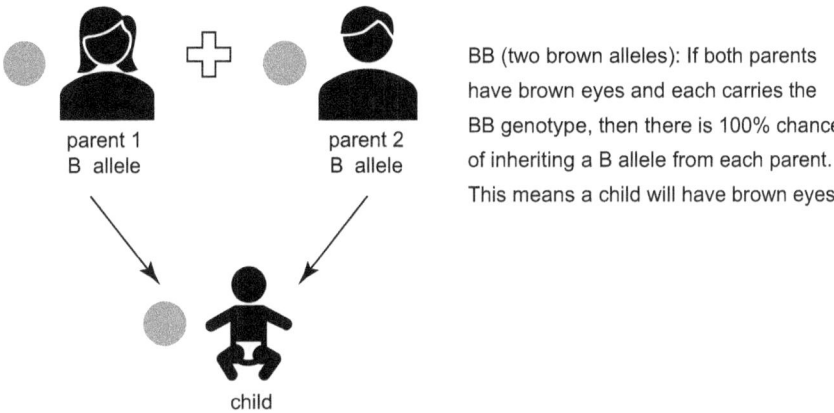

Figure 5.3 The use of text, pictures and colours enhances the meaning of passages.

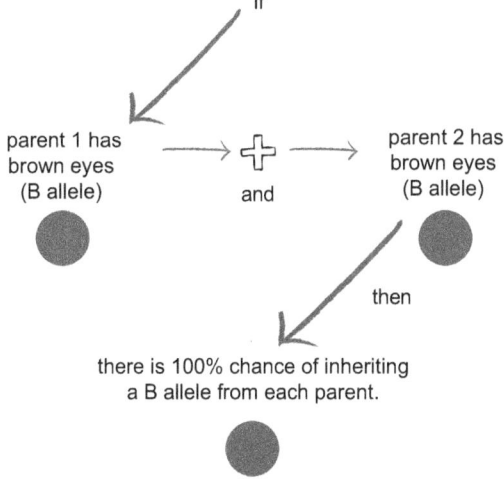

Figure 5.4 Alternative ways of presenting the same content might allow for better comprehension.

86   Striking the balance

The Russian Revolution of 1917 brought about profound and far-reaching consequences. The revolution marked the end of centuries of Tsarist autocracy, paving the way for the establishment of the world's first socialist state, the Soviet Union. The revolution, however, triggered a civil war between Bolshevik and anti-Bolshevik forces, resulting in widespread destruction and loss of life. The socialist government implemented policies aimed at addressing social and economic inequalities, providing essential services like healthcare and education to the population. Land reforms were introduced and women's rights saw significant improvement. The transition to a socialist economy proved challenging, leading to economic disruptions. Political repression was enforced and individual liberties were curtailed in the name of the collective interest. Additionally, famine and food shortages plagued the nation during the Civil War, causing widespread hunger and suffering among the population.

The Russian Revolution of 1917 brought about profound and far-reaching consequences.

positive 👍

The revolution marked the end of centuries of Tsarist autocracy, paving the way for the establishment of the world's first socialist state, the Soviet Union

political consequences

The socialist government implemented policies aimed at addressing social inequalities, providing essential services like healthcare and education to the population.

social consequences

Land reforms were introduced.

economic consequences

negative 👎

The revolution, however, triggered a civil war between Bolshevik and anti-Bolshevik forces, resulting in widespread destruction and loss of life.

political consequences

The transition to a socialist economy proved challenging, leading to economic disruptions.

economic consequences

Political repression was enforced and individual liberties were curtailed in the name of the collective interest.

political consequences

Famine and food shortages plagued the nation during the Civil War, causing widespread hunger and suffering among the population.

economic consequences

Figure 5.5 Modification can be used to present longer passages.

Fiction texts

The decision between simplification and easification presents a particularly challenging dilemma when dealing with literary works. Various degrees of simplification and easification can be deemed appropriate, depending on factors such as students' English proficiency levels, background knowledge, time of enrolment during the academic year and the allocated duration for the study of a specific text. In practical terms, it is not feasible, for instance, to meticulously examine each unfamiliar word in a 19th-century novel, focusing on its meaning, morphology and use in diverse contexts. Similarly, dedicating extensive time to exploring all cultural or historical references, especially if they bear minimal relevance to the primary focus of a lesson or unit, would be excessively time-consuming. Such an approach could overwhelm students and lead them to believe that every minute detail is indispensable for comprehending the novel and the lesson and achieving success.

Let us consider the opening paragraph of Daphne du Maurier's *Rebecca* (2018), which may be deemed a challenging text for multilingual learners due to its complex and occasionally intricate sentence structure, less common or infrequently used vocabulary, a variety of past tenses indicating the order of events and numerous cultural references. The original first paragraph is as follows:

> Last night I dreamt I went to Manderley again. It seemed to me I stood by the iron gate leading to the drive, and for a while I could not enter, for the way was barred to me. There was a padlock and a chain upon the gate. I called in my dream to the lodge-keeper, and had no answer, and peering closer through the rusted spokes of the gate I saw that the lodge was uninhabited.

The revised version of the four sentences might be as follows:

> Last night, I dreamt I went to Manderley again. I stood by the iron gate, but it was locked with a padlock and chain. I called for the caretaker, but there was no answer. Looking through the rusty spokes, I saw the house was empty.

In the original paragraph, the sentences are longer and more complex with multiple clauses and phrases. In the simplified paragraphs, the sentences are shorter and more straightforward, containing only one or two clauses. Similarly, the original version uses a slightly more varied and formal vocabulary, including phrases like 'seemed to me', 'for a while', 'barred to me', 'peering closer'. The simplified paragraph uses simpler and more common words and phrases like 'but', 'locked' and 'looking'. Overall, the simplified paragraph maintains the essence of the original content while making it easier to read and understand.

The simplistic account, as exemplified below, results in an exceedingly elementary summary of the paragraph, both in terms of vocabulary and grammar. However, for some students, such as those with little or disrupted previous education on literacy in their first language or newcomers to both English and the text itself, such a streamlined version may

88 *Striking the balance*

serve as an accessible entry point. Instead of presenting students with a highly complex passage filled with unfamiliar vocabulary and intricate grammatical structures that could further hinder comprehension, the provided text below, to a certain extent, facilitates students' active participation in the lesson, rather than overwhelming them and potentially causing frustration.

> Last night, I had a dream. I went to Manderley again. I stood by the gate but it was locked. I called for someone. No answer. The gate was old. The house was empty.

Simplification may appear **suitable under certain circumstances**, but it potentially raises several challenging issues that may prove difficult to overcome. Firstly, the process of rewriting, simplifying and modifying entire books or extended passages is undoubtedly time-consuming. Furthermore, it necessitates the use of different texts and documents by some students and the teacher, leading to confusion and logistical complexities in managing a classroom setting. Moreover, students using the simplified or overly simplistic version of the text would miss out on the opportunity to engage in literary analysis on par with their peers. For instance, if a lesson centres on the author's creation of the atmosphere in the opening paragraph and crucial words such as 'peering', 'barred', 'rusty spokes' and 'uninhabited' are omitted, students face a disadvantage.

Easification devices for literary texts

Easification, as a method of enhancing text accessibility without substantial alterations to its vocabulary, grammar and form presents a more favourable solution. This approach exposes students to the same literary resources as their peers, while preserving the genre's essential lexical and syntactic features. Nonetheless, easification employs specific techniques or devices to scaffold text comprehension, including:

1. previewing or summarising overarching ideas presented in the text.
2. Explaining culturally or historically relevant concepts.
3. dividing the text into logical sections.
4. identifying and explaining key vocabulary through synonyms, definitions, visuals, morphological analysis, etc.
5. highlighting and explaining language functions that drive text cohesion.

Dividing the text into sections and determining the essential words and phrases crucial for comprehending the text can be done prior to the lesson. Subsequently, the teacher can proactively take measures to either directly incorporate visuals into the text, if feasible, or prepare supplementary materials like a PowerPoint slide or handout. This is how the opening of Rebecca could appear when easification devices are implemented.

Striking the balance 89

• **Preview overarching ideas**

The extract from 'Rebecca' focuses on the narrator's journey
along the driveway as she approaches Manderley.
The driveway is twisting, overgrown and covered
with weeds and bushes.

Have you ever seen a forgotten driveway? Where?
What did it look like?
How did it make you feel?

Figure 5.6 Improving student comprehension can be facilitated by offering concise summaries and connecting them to students' personal experiences.

2. Explain culturally or historically relevant concepts

Manderley is a country estate. A wealthy family owns the land and the
house is run by a lot of staff.

Figure 5.7 Comprehending cultural references and nuances is crucial for understanding texts originating from diverse cultures.

Numerous academic studies (Alexander, Kulikowich and Schulze, 1994; Hirsch, 2003) have emphasised **the significance of background knowledge in comprehension** of a text, as exemplified by the influential and frequently cited work of Recht and Leslie (Recht and Leslie, 1988). Background knowledge, referring to one's understanding of the world and specific domains, offers contextual support, enabling readers to establish connections between new information and their existing knowledge, thereby facilitating a deeper comprehension of the author's meaning and intent. The absence of such contextual information may pose challenges in grasping the relevance and significance of the presented text.

90 *Striking the balance*

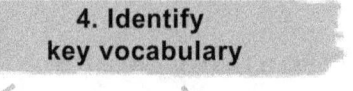 **4. Identify key vocabulary**

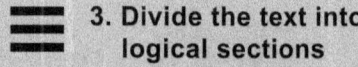 **3. Divide the text into logical sections**

the iron gate

a padlock and a chain

peering closer

the lodge was uninhabited

forlorn = sad

the twisting and turning drive

branch of a tree

insidious = sly, secretive

<u>Last night</u> I dreamt I went to Manderley again. It seemed to me I stood by **the iron gate** leading to the drive, and <u>for a while</u> I could not enter, for the way was barred to me. There was **a padlock and a chain** upon the gate.

I called in my dream to the lodge-keeper, and had no answer, and **peering closer** through the rusted spokes of the gate I saw that **the lodge was** un**inhabited.** No smoke came from the chimney, and the little lattice windows gaped **forlorn.** <u>Then,</u> like all dreamers, I was possessed of a sudden with supernatural powers and passed like a spirit through the barrier before me.

The drive wound away in front of me, **twisting and turning** as it had always done, but as I advanced I was aware that a change had come upon it; it was narrow and un kept, not the drive that we had known. <u>At first</u> I was puzzled and did not understand, and it was <u>only when</u> I bent my head to avoid the low swinging **branch of a tree** that I realised that had happened. Nature had come into her own again and, little by little, in her stealthy, **insidious** way had encroached upon the drive with long, tenacious fingers. The woods, always a menace even in the past, had triumphed <u>in the end</u>.

 5. highlight language functions

1. g a t e

2. g a t e h o u s e

3. d r i v e t o M a n d e r l e y

Figure 5.8 A number of easification devices applied to a literary text.

To enhance reading comprehension, several strategies are recommended. Firstly, previewing the main ideas or briefly summarising the key points of the text grants students insight into its primary themes. This initial scaffold lays the foundation upon which further detail can be incorporated as the text unfolds. Additionally, encouraging questions that relate to the students' own experiences on the subject matter enhances their ability to reinforce their existing scheme of knowledge. Such an approach fosters confidence and minimises stress or frustration when encountering unfamiliar words or phrases during the first reading of the text. Secondly, some students may already be familiar with certain cultural references integral to comprehension and contextualising the text. Explicitly explaining content like the country estate of Manderley and providing visual aids, such as photographs and short videos, better prepares learners for engaging with lexically and grammatically complex passages. By doing so, students are equipped with the necessary background information, contributing to a more comprehensive and meaningful reading experience.

In cases where the text permits, it is beneficial to organise it into coherent sections that signify shifts in topics, the progression of events or the sequence of expected elements. In this specific instance, once students have gained familiarity with the concepts related to a country estate, it becomes helpful to divide the text into paragraphs that outline explicit aspects of the estate. Additionally, the inclusion of pictures serves to represent key tangible and abstract notions. Furthermore, the opportunity arises to delve into word morphology, such as examining the prefix 'un' signifying 'not'. Moreover, students' attention is directed towards temporal phrases, which indicate the chronological order of events, enabling them to monitor their comprehension throughout the passage.

Easification, as distinct from simplification, of a text does not compromise the integrity and authenticity of the original content. While certain manipulations, like organising the text into logical sections, may be beneficial, extensive modifications can lead to altering the text beyond recognition. To effectively apply the features of a specific genre, it is crucial to recognise and analyse them, enabling students to incorporate these aspects into their own writing (Bhatia, 1983). Excessive simplification, as in the case of the opening passage of *Rebecca*, risks diluting the distinctive characteristics of Gothic literature, such as its atmosphere of mystery, tension and the use of nature as a reflective element. Easification, however, enhances text accessibility for multilingual learners while preserving the original symbolism and impact through the unchanged lexical and grammatical choices of the author.

Summary

Why?

The use of simplification and simplified texts:

- enhances comprehension for students who are in the early stages of learning English.
- promotes an inclusive learning environment for students as they can access and actively participate in mainstream lessons.

- allows multilingual learners who are new to English to study the same content as their peers without feeling overwhelmed by linguistic complexities.
- sempower multilingual students to engage with the material independently as they can gradually build their language skills while simultaneously gaining subject knowledge.

How?

1. identify key concepts and ideas that underpin the significance of the text and ensure their continued presence within the simplified version.
2. substitute unfamiliar, complex or less frequently used words with more commonly used vocabulary or provide a synonym for them; do not replace subject-specific words which are crucial to understanding the topic.
3. use shorter sentences by breaking long and complex ones into more concise ones.
4. use active voice if possible as using passive voice can be more confusing and less straightforward.
5. present ideas in bullet points or lists.
6. use visual aids in the form of pictures, graphs, diagrams, etc.
7. ensure that the logical flow of the text is preserved.

Levels

A-C:

- the vocabulary and sentence structure will vary based on students' language proficiency.
- gradually increase the complexity of syntax and vocabulary.
- it is important to ensure that students are exposed and interact with the original versions of texts too.

Why?

Easification:

- students are exposed to and engage with the same texts as their peers.
- original texts, with easification devices, maintain academic rigour and do not compromise the content.
- learners encounter vocabulary and sentence structures that are characteristic of specific genres and sub-genres.
- contextual clues (when appropriate) are provided, enabling students to establish connections with their own personal experiences.
- the necessity to generate multiple versions of resources is circumvented.

How?

1. identify key concepts and ideas that underlie the text's significance.
2. provide a succinct summary of the primary idea(s).
3. identify and explain key vocabulary relevant to the text's overarching message, encompassing definitions, synonyms and visual aids.
4. segment the text into coherent sections that enhance the overall message's logical flow.
5. demonstrate oral reading of the text and articulate cognitive processes during the chunking and analysis of complex sentences and inter-sentence cohesion.

Levels

A-E:

- students who are beginners or in the early stages of developing English language proficiency levels might benefit from close directions with regard to key vocabulary and the purpose of the text.
- explanations of a wider range of words (apart from the identified key vocabulary) might be helpful.
- if possible, provide the text in students' first languages or assign research tasks pertaining to the topic in their first language prior to reading the text in English.

References

Alexander, P., Kulikowich, J. and Schulze, S. 1994. How Subject-Matter Knowledge Affects Recall and Interest. *American Educational Research Journal*, **31**(2), pp. 313-337.

Bhatia, V. K. 1983. Simplification v. Easification: The Case of Legal Texts. *Applied Linguistics*, **4**(1), pp. 42-54.

Bhatia, V. K. 1993. *Analysing Genre: Language Use in Professional Setting*. New York: Longman.

Billings, E. and Walqui, A. n.d. *De-Mystifying Complex Texts: What are "Complex" Texts and How Can We Ensure ELLs and MLs Can Access Them?* [Online] Accessed 11 August 2023. Available from: https://www.nysed.gov/bilingual-ed/topic-brief-3-de-mystifying-complex-texts-what-are-complex-texts-and-how-can-we-ensure.

Du Maurier, D. 2018. *Rebecca*. London: Virago Press.

Hirsch, E. D. 2003. Reading Comprehension Requires Knowledge – of Words and the World. *American Educator*, **27**(1), pp. 10-23.

Krashen, S. D. 1982. *Principles and Practice in Second Language Acquisition*. Oxford: Pergamon Press.

Recht, D. R. and Leslie, L. 1988. Effect of Prior Knowledge on Good and Poor Readers' Memory of Text. *Journal of Educational Psychology*, **80**(1), pp. 16-20.

Widdowson, H. G. 1978. *Teaching Language as Communication*. London: Oxford University Press.

6 'One to bring them all'
The multifaceted worlds of writing for EAL students

Although not exclusively, writing is one of the strongest indicators of a student's academic success as many exams are writing-based and require high proficiency in literacy (Harmer, 2004; Lemov, 2021). It is, therefore, crucial for the students to be able to produce grammatically, lexically and stylistically appropriate texts. On top of that, many researchers and educators highlight the importance of selecting and writing in an appropriate genre and maintaining its features (Cameron, 2003; Harmer, 2004; Thornbury, 2006). Writing, without a doubt, is recognised as a complex skill and requires mastering, or at least being able to sufficiently perform a number of subskills. Researchers and linguists highlight that some of the subskills are performed automatically and mechanically by proficient writers, for example forming letters (Thornbury, 2006; Harmer, 2004). Others, such as planning and re-vising longer pieces of writing require more conscious thought. Additionally, apart from expressing themselves with grammatical and lexical accuracy, proficient writers are aware of and understand different registers: they comprehend that language choices depend on the situation they find themselves in. Experienced writers will also make suitable linguistic choices based on the field they are writing in and will adjust their writing with regards to the subject or discipline (Derewienka and Jones, 2016; Cummins, 2021). Learners, therefore, need a wide range of linguistic, social and cultural knowledge in order to write successfully in English.

What makes writing particularly intriguing is that it serves as the perfect **platform to integrate all language skills** seamlessly. In this chapter, we delve into the intricate art of writing, recognising the unique challenges it presents for EAL learners. While writing can be a formidable task, it stands as a remarkable opportunity to integrate various language skills. We emphasise that writing is not a solitary skill; it is intricately connected to reading, speaking, vocabulary and grammar. The activities presented in this chapter are carefully designed to provide ample opportunities for students to develop a range of language skills. By engaging in these activities, students will not only enhance their writing abilities but also experience a significant spillover effect on their other language skills. These activities will encourage students to articulate their thoughts and ideas aloud, fostering the development of speaking and pronunciation. Furthermore, as they work on structuring sentences and paragraphs, they will naturally reinforce their understanding of grammar.

DOI: 10.4324/9781003386810-6

Why might writing be challenging for EAL learners?

There are many similarities between the process of producing a text in students' first languages and in a second language. However, alongside the similarities, there are some notable differences too. Hyland (Hyland, 2003) points out that the most obvious difference is the writer's command of grammar and vocabulary in a new language. Grammatical knowledge refers to the understanding of the rules of language that govern the formation of sentences and the precise use of punctuation, while lexical knowledge pertains to the writer's vocabulary and their ability to use words accurately and effectively. Proficient language users and writers have mastered the use of punctuation and grammatical structures and have a large body of vocabulary at their disposal. Cameron (Cameron, 2003) points out that English as an Additional Language learners in mainstream English schools often struggle with maintaining the features of a genre and lexical and grammatical mistakes hinder the clarity of the texts produced. Academic writing, which often requires complex structures, such as noun phrases (for example 'food scarcity'), nouns derived from verbs (such as 'justification' from 'justify'), the use of passive voice ('The temperature *was measured* at regular intervals') or the use of subordination, appositive phrases or adjunct clauses ('In 1066, William the Conqueror, a Norman Duke, successfully invaded England, culminating in the Battle of Hastings, which marked a pivotal moment in English history') (Wong Filmore, 2009). Writing in academic contexts, therefore, often requires a deeper understanding of the language, including vocabulary, syntax and academic discourse. Professor Cummin's work on the distinction between BICS and CALP has had a significant impact on the field of language education, highlighting the need for teachers to provide appropriate support and instruction to help students develop both sets of language skills to excel academically (Cummins, 1984, 2021).

Multilingual learners who are beginners or at the intermediate levels of English language acquisition might struggle with producing grammatically and lexically accurate texts as the lexicon they have been exposed to might still be limited. Similarly, there might be a limited number and scope of grammatical structures they have practised and mastered. Cameron (Cameron, 2003) notes that students who attend mainstream English schools and are learning English, often struggle with consistent use of past tenses, noun-pronoun agreement, collocations and the use of appropriate words to express themselves with clarity. The main issue for teaching and learning is the consideration and careful planning for vocabulary and grammar that will be required during a lesson. There is a danger that some multilingual learners will face cognitive overload if trying to use and remember too many complex constructions. On the other hand, their writing might lack the expected details and clarity if they only resort to the structures they know and have mastered.

Many multilingual learners are proficient writers in their first languages and, if they attended secondary school before being admitted to an English-speaking school, might have well-developed academic writing skills in different subjects. The context of the new culture and the context of some situations might not be, however, familiar to them. Sharples (Sharples, 2021) points out that multilingual students in English-medium schools might have less implicit knowledge about writing certain types of texts. These features should be taught explicitly, modelled and explained so that students can learn how to adapt their writing style, tone and structure depending on the genre they are working with. Although on the surface many features will be similar, in some countries academic writing might differ in terms of the structure of essays, employing more narrative style similar to storytelling or greater emphasis on qualitative data. Similarly, learners may refer to and rely on their different educational backgrounds and the amount of expertise on a given topic when completing any writing task. When writing, in particular with regards to disciplinary discourses, the students need to have relevant knowledge about the topic or theme (Hyland, 2004). Usually these topics are prescribed by the school, syllabus or national curriculum. As Cameron (2003) points out, students who speak English as their second language, often approach writing tasks with not enough content knowledge and that significantly impacts their ability to plan extended pieces of writing. The teacher's role is to build the appropriate cognitive schema so that students can write meaningful and coherent texts. Lessons need to be planned expertly so that both linguistic knowledge, which includes how to write in different genres and content knowledge, develop simultaneously.

The activities outlined below showcase how the different elements of writing, including grammar, vocabulary and genre, can be taught in mainstream lessons. These tasks could be used with students who are at different levels of the English language proficiency and many of them should be treated as a temporary scaffold.

Substitution tables

To address the issue of varying levels of lexical and grammatical proficiency that new to English or early acquisition learners might have, using substitution tables is an effective strategy. This is an example of a strategy where learners manipulate models provided by the teacher: they choose one word/expression from each column in order to produce a full sentence. As Hyland (Hyland, 2003) highlights, substitution tables ensure that **the text produced is grammatically and lexically appropriate**. Since accuracy and clarity are some of the main criteria of writing, learners are provided with fixed or semi-fixed expressions, and a limited number of choices which results in producing, most likely, error-free writing. This type of product approach works well with beginner to intermediate classes as the students are not overwhelmed with too many choices and can practise lexical and grammatical items with a certain degree of predictability. Substitution tables, however, can be quite restrictive and, if used frequently, will prohibit students from constructing sentences independently. They are effective when we consider novice writers as they provide the right amount of scaffolding and guidance. It is considerate to remove them or use them sparingly in order to develop learners' independence.

Substitution tables can be easily adapted by adding visuals, a space for students to add their own ideas or there could be more columns added if students are working on longer and more complex utterances.

'One to bring them all' 97

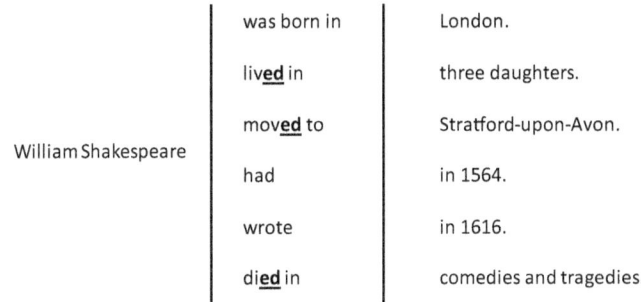

	was born in	London.
	liv**ed** in	three daughters.
	mov**ed** to	Stratford-upon-Avon.
William Shakespeare	had	in 1564.
	wrote	in 1616.
	di**ed** in	comedies and tragedies.

Figure 6.1 A three-column substitution table for assessing students' knowledge and emphasising the use of past tense.

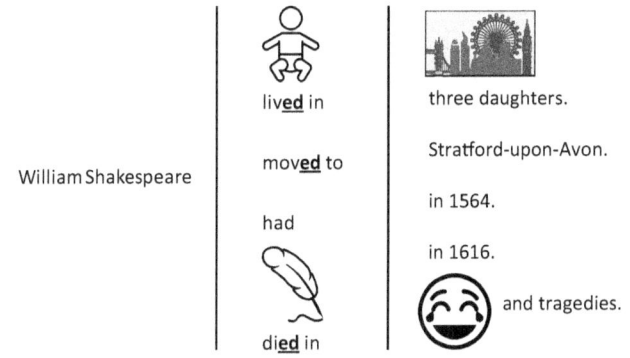

Figure 6.2 Substitution tables give the flexibility to include visuals.

It is important that by the use of substitution tables we amplify and allow students to practise a key aspect of grammar, vocabulary or sentence structure. It is also an effective way to check students' understanding without overwhelming them with the requirement to think about the appropriate and correct way of verbalising the answers. The activity in Figure 6.3 focuses on recalling key knowledge about the structure of the earth and allows

The c_____			semi-solid or m_____ rock.
The m_____		is made of	iron and nickel.
The c_____			s_____ rock.

Figure 6.3 Substitution tables should highlight key grammatical points for effective language learning.

'One to bring them all'

for controlled practice of the passive voice. Students use the three words 'is made of' as one phrase, therefore the extra challenge of creating the grammatical utterance is alleviated and learners can focus on factual information.

In some instances, the key focus and aim of a substitution table could be practising **one aspect of grammar**, for example using verbs in the second form, or in the past simple. The level of challenge is raised as students are tasked with finishing the sentences with their own ideas.

The example provided can also be highly beneficial when introducing and teaching students about subtle distinctions between specific words and expressions. Students can be encouraged and guided in the process of selecting and matching different verbs and expressions from the table to explore how these choices can influence readers' perceptions. It is important to recognise that the words chosen in these sentences can subtly shape how readers interpret the author's purpose and communication style. Depending on the specific word used, readers may attribute varying degrees of intention, dedication, clarity or formality to the author's message. Students should understand that even though the sentences share a common core idea, they differ in terms of the nuances that convey the author's approach to conveying their intent. For instance, opting for the verb 'aims' suggests a deliberate and focused effort by the author, whereas selecting the verb 'attempts' implies that the author is making an effort but doesn't guarantee success. Assigning tasks to students in which they compose sentences using different words and provide explanations for their choices will heighten their awareness that slight variations in language can convey distinct shades of meaning.

It can also be beneficial to introduce substitution tables for focusing on parts of speech and sentence syntax. The table in Figure 6.5 illustrates the word order and labels each part of

The author	aims to endeavours to strives to attempts	communicate express convey get across elucidate	their intention by their purpose through their meaning through their message by their intent through	

Figure 6.4 Substitution tables allow for a great level of flexibility.

adverb / adverbial phrase (how?)	pronoun (who?)	verb (what happened?)	article	adjective (what type? which ones?)	noun (what?)	preposition (where?)	noun (what?)
Suddenly,	I	noticed	a	sinister	shadow	behind	___ .
All of a sudden,		spotted		dark		Next to	___ .
_____		saw		monstrous		above	___ .
_____		became aware of		long		_____	___ .

Figure 6.5 Thanks to substitution tables we can focus on key grammatical or lexical items.

speech. In English lessons, the identification of various parts of speech is often necessary; this metalinguistic knowledge can be valuable, enabling students to construct sentences with greater precision and clarity.

Summary

Why?

Substitution tables:

- allow for controlled grammar and vocabulary practice.
- focus on students' precision in writing.
- draw students' attention to key grammatical patterns and structures.
- can be easily adapted to suit the lessons' requirements and the students' language levels.

How?

1. substitution tables should be clear and easy to navigate. Organise them in a user-friendly manner, such as in columns or rows.
2. select, concentrate on and emphasise key grammatical structures or vocabulary.
3. highlight grammatical or lexical patterns. It may be a beneficial idea to treat certain phrases and expressions as lexical units rather than individual words.
4. introduce some flexibility by incorporating gap-fill exercises or open-ended sentence constructions.

Levels

A-C (New to English - Developing Competence):

- substitution tables can serve as a scaffold to support students' language development, especially when the emphasis is on grammatical and lexical accuracy and precision.

- they are somewhat constraining and may not be suitable for students at more advanced levels of English proficiency. Nevertheless, they can prove effective when introducing nuanced meanings of vocabulary or complex, less commonly used grammatical structures.

Graphic organisers

The clarity, cohesiveness and coherence of students' writing is often achieved thanks to planning. Planning and drafting writing refers to the very initial stages of a writing process during which writers collect, organise and expand their ideas. Many researchers and linguists highlight the fact that effective writers plan, or at least think about their writing and approach it as a recursive or cyclical process rather than a linear activity (Gibbons, 2015; Thornbury, 2006; Hayland, 2004; Harmer, 2004). Graphic organisers are incredibly helpful tools for planning writing because they offer several advantages that can significantly enhance the writing process. They are useful to multilingual as well as monolingual students because of:

- **visual organisation:** graphic organisers provide a visual representation of ideas and their relationships. This visual structure makes it easier for students to see the overall organisation of their work. It helps them plan and structure their thoughts, leading to more coherent writing.
- **clarity and focus:** by breaking down complex concepts or ideas into smaller, manageable components, graphic organisers help writers clarify their thinking. They can see the logical progression of their argument or the narrative flow, which makes it easier to maintain focus on the main message.
- **enhanced understanding:** when students use graphic organisers, they often need to think critically about how different parts of their writing connect. This process deepens their understanding of the topic.
- **revision assistance:** graphic organisers make it easier for students to identify areas in their writing that may need revision. The visual layout highlights gaps, inconsistencies or logical flaws in the text, making the revision process more efficient.
- **versatility:** graphic organisers are flexible and adaptable to various writing tasks. Whether it is narrative writing, persuasive essays, research reports or creative writing, there are graphic organiser templates suitable for each type of writing.
- **language support:** graphic organisers can serve as language support tools for multilingual learners. This is the perfect example where planning in terms of the content can be easily enhanced and supported by the use of appropriate language structures.

The final point is of particular significance when considering multilingual learners, as proficient writers must carefully consider both the content and the manner in which they compose a text. Students should possess a solid understanding of the subject they are addressing, while also having a command of the appropriate language structures that enable them to express their ideas clearly.

'One to bring them all' 101

Let's examine two versions of the same graphic organiser. It can be employed in various subjects, such as history lessons, to assist students in planning an extended piece of writing that concentrates on the causes and reasons behind a historical event. The first version acts as a visual aid, aiding students in the organisation of their thoughts and ideas. By structuring their responses within these visual frameworks, students develop a more coherent grasp of the logical flow and interconnections between key points within the content. Consequently, this process enhances their capability to present a well-structured response or essay.

The linguistic support provided alongside these graphic organisers equips students with the necessary vocabulary, language structures and transitional phrases required to effectively express their thoughts. This **linguistic scaffolding** not only aids learners in articulating their ideas more effectively but also cultivates language development and proficiency. It serves as a scaffold that teachers can adapt to ensure that students have ideas and can express them coherently. Consider how much more accessible and inclusive the task becomes when linguistic support and guidance are available. By incorporating these elements, we promote

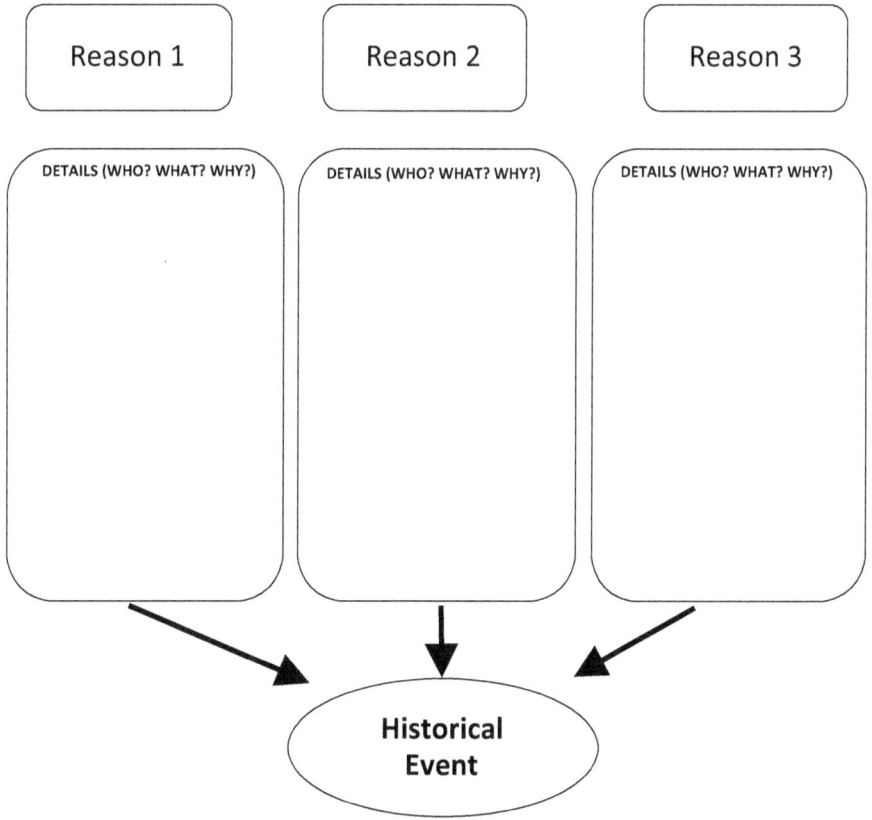

Figure 6.6 Graphic organisers help visually structure and organise ideas, enhancing clarity and coherence in the written work.

'One to bring them all'

language proficiency and enhance students' ability to convey complex ideas with clarity. Additionally, language scaffolds bolster confidence and reduce apprehension, motivating students to tackle more advanced writing tasks, which are essential for academic success.

It is imperative to recognise that both content and language are of equal importance in the learning process for EAL learners. Treating these two elements with parity is a fundamental concept, as they are inextricably linked, and their interplay profoundly influences a student's ability to grasp and convey complex ideas. This equilibrium demands that we structure educational resources differently, with both elements accorded the same level of attention and consideration. Such an approach ensures that learners not only acquire the

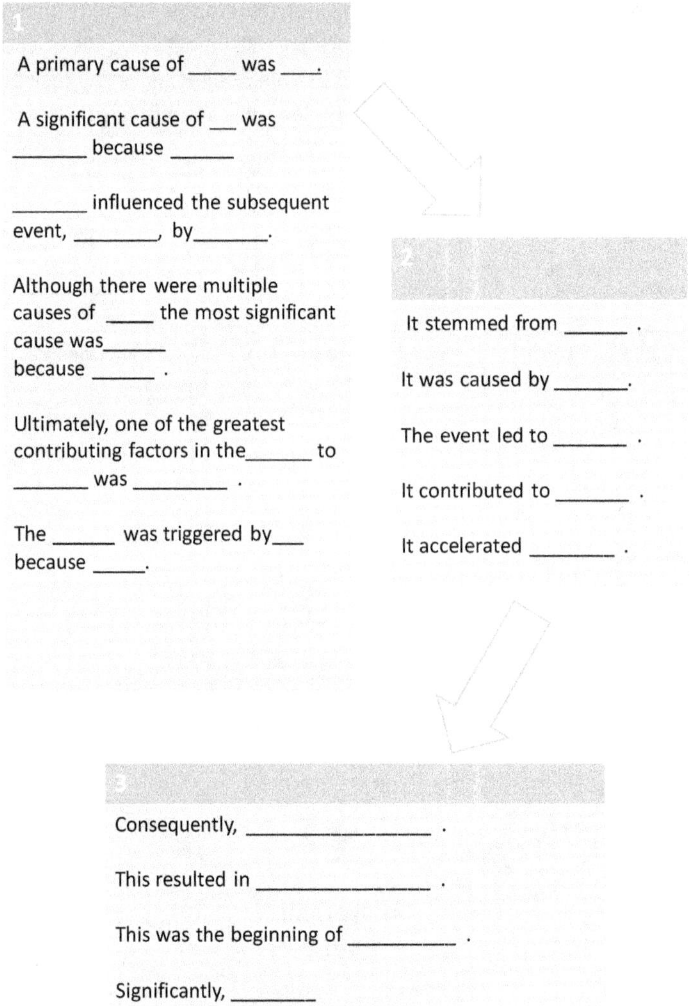

1

A primary cause of _____ was _____.

A significant cause of ___ was _____ because _____

_____ influenced the subsequent event, _____, by_____.

Although there were multiple causes of _____ the most significant cause was_____ because _____.

Ultimately, one of the greatest contributing factors in the_____ to _____ was _____.

The _____ was triggered by___ because _____.

2

It stemmed from _____.

It was caused by _____.

The event led to _____.

It contributed to _____.

It accelerated _____.

3

Consequently, _____.

This resulted in _____.

This was the beginning of _____.

Significantly, _____

Figure 6.7 Scaffolding and language planning are equally as crucial as content planning.

'One to bring them all' 103

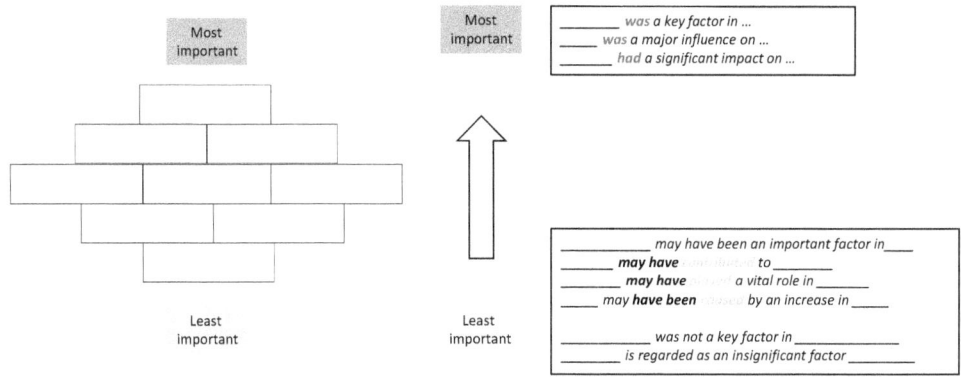

Figure 6.8 Content and language should be equally important when designing materials for EAL learners.

subject matter but also the linguistic skills necessary to complete a task. By **planning for content and language with equal emphasis**, we provide a supportive and inclusive environment that enables multilingual learners to achieve academic success.

Summary

Why?

Graphic organisers:

- enhance comprehension as they allow to organise complex information into more manageable units.
- help structure ideas and relationships between concepts.
- when combined with language scaffolds allow students articulate their ideas with clarity and precision.

How?

1. model how to fill a graphic organiser or show examples of completed organisers, discussing how to fill them out effectively. Model the process for organising ideas and using appropriate language structures.
2. encourage students to use all their linguistic repertoire and ask students to take notes and write in their first languages.
3. if appropriate for a task, encourage collaboration where students can use graphic organisers together to share and refine ideas. This fosters language practice and mutual support.
4. adjust the complexity of graphic organisers and the language support accordingly.
5. incorporate graphic organisers into regular lessons, assignments and assessments to reinforce their use and help learners become more proficient in structuring their thoughts and expressing themselves effectively.

Levels

A-E:

- knowledge retrieval tasks as part of the preparation.
- tasks can be completed independently or in pairs/groups.
- exemplar texts are providing and explained by the teacher.
- sentence stems are provided to support learners in constructing their sentences.
- visuals are provided to aid comprehension.

Parallel writing

Modelling writing for multilingual learners in an effective instructional strategy that incorporates examples and provides step- by-step guidance. Parallel writing, as **a structured and controlled approach**, allows students of varying proficiency levels to create a cohesive text on a given topic. It is a good idea to introduce the task towards the end of a lesson or a unit, ensuring that students are already familiar with the content covered in the session.

In parallel writing, students are assigned **the task of emulating a model text**, developing their own writing based on a similar theme whilst using the same grammatical structures. The model text serves as a guide to be followed, emphasising the importance of not merely copying it word by word. Students must understand the content, structure and grammar of the text in order to successfully apply relevant grammatical rules. To support parallel writing tasks, visual aids, key words or phrases and sentence starters can be provided. These resources assist students in formulating their ideas and initiating their writing process.

Parallel sentences

Parallel writing can support sentence and paragraph construction. The two examples below demonstrate how the strategy of imitating a model text can enhance students' writing skills and provide **controlled practice** where both content and language are equally important.

In this geography activity, students are tasked with describing the location of the two cities. The necessary information is provided in the table, which can be further adapted for students to fill in the appropriate rows with headings such as 'continent', 'country', 'region' etc. After providing a model sentence, learners write their own sentence focusing on the correct use of prepositions of place. Multilingual learners often struggle with these prepositions as they may rely on literal translation from their first languages into English. In addition to highlighting the prominent aspects of the grammatical structures used in the given sentence, we allow all students, including those at earlier stages of learning, even those who are at the earlier stages of learning English, to construct complex sentences. By modelling sentences and guiding students through controlled practice, we aim to prevent the

'One to bring them all' 105

London	A	Edinburgh	B
1.Europe		1.Europe	
2.England, UK		2.Scotland, UK	
3.south-east		3.east	
4.River Thames		4.Water of Leith	
5.Greater London		5.Central Belt	
6.area: 1,573 square km		6.area: 275 square km	

Figure 6.9 The essential information required for the writing task may either be provided in advance or used as a retrieval exercise.

repetition of starting each sentence *'It is _____.'*. Instead, students are encouraged to use appositive phrases (sentence 2) and fronted adverbials (sentence 3).

1A London: London is in the continent of Europe.
1B Edinburgh: _____.
2A London: London, the capital city of England, is located in the southeastern part of the UK.
2B Edinburgh: _____.
3A London: Situated on the banks of the River Thames, it occupies a strategic position in the Greater London region.
3B Edinburgh: _____.
4A London: The urban area of London is approximately 1,572 square kilometres.
4B Edinburgh: _____.

Parallel paragraphs

The example in Figure 6.10 provides an opportunity to engage with longer pieces of writing and focuses on the description of plant and animal cells. Students are provided with a labelled diagram of a plant cell. As a knowledge retrieval task, students could be asked to label the diagram and provide the functions of each element.

Following that, a short text is provided which describes the components of a plant cell and their functions. During the read-aloud stage, the teacher comments on specific vocabulary choices, text structure and key grammatical points.

Once students have familiarised themselves with the conceptual and linguistic requirements of the task, they can begin planning for their own independent work with clear guidance and a model to follow. The level of challenge can be controlled based on the amount of

106 'One to bring them all'

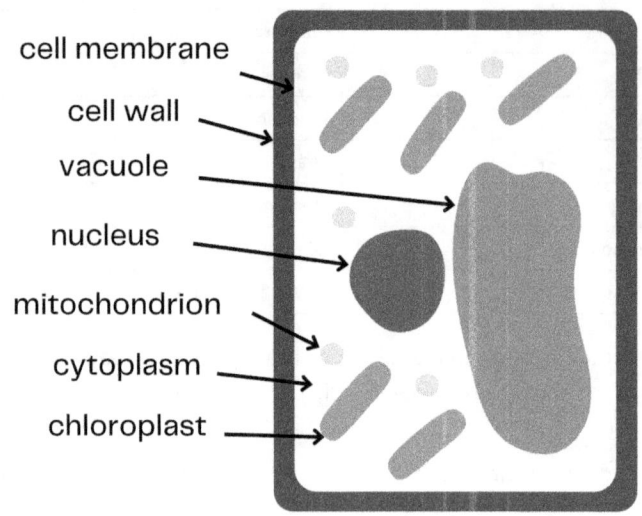

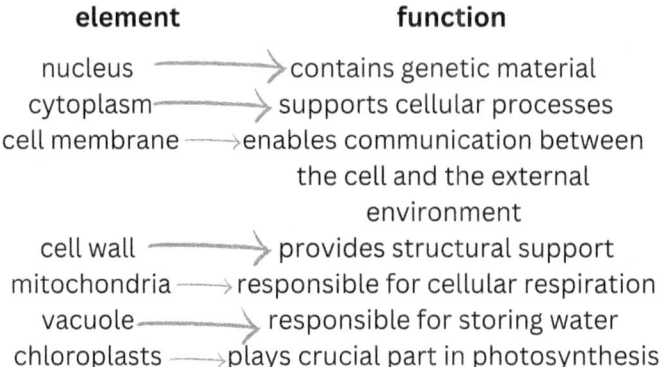

Figure 6.10 During the preparation stage, students could be provided with the key information necessary to complete the written task.

information students are asked to recall from memory. Some of the scaffolding tasks during the planning stage could involve labelling the diagram with or without the first letters provided, matching the names of the elements with their functions. A short paired, group or teacher-led discussion could follow this task allowing students the opportunity to check and edit their answers. This also provides learners a chance to rehearse their answers orally whilst attempting to incorporate the key linguistic features mentioned during the analysis of the model text.

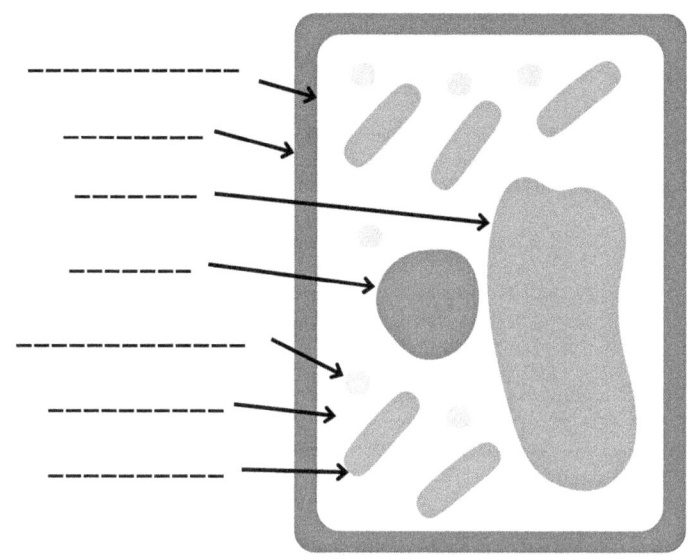

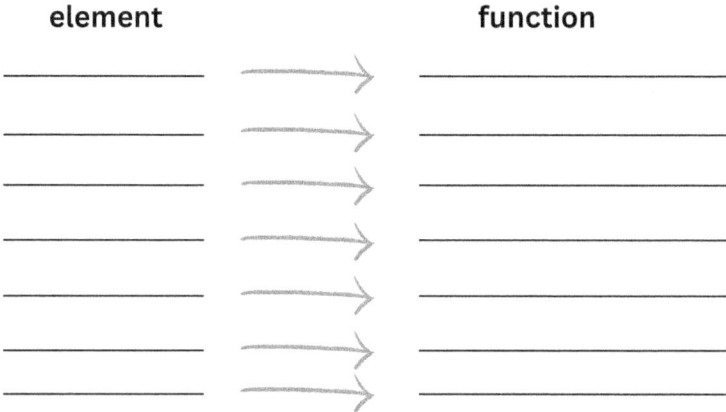

Figure 6.11 As part of a preparation and retrieval task, students could be prompted to independently recall essential information.

The next stage is for students to independently write the text, closely imitating the structures and the highlighted grammatical structures, such as the use of the passive voice and the relative pronoun 'which'. Further support in the form of sentence starters could be provided. Students' attention should be drawn to effectively utilise the appropriate structures.

108   'One to bring them all'

explain: what is a plant cell? list: all the key elements	A plant cell is a fundamental unit of plant organisms. The plant cell **comprises** a <u>nucleus, cytoplasm, cell wall, mitochondria, vacuole and chloroplasts.</u>	**comprises:** made up of, consists of
name: 1 element and explain its function	At the core of the plant cell lies <u>the nucleus</u> *which* contains the genetic materials. The cell's interior **is filled** with <u>the cytoplasm</u> *which* supports numerous cellular processes. The plant cell **is enclosed** by <u>the cell membrane</u> *which* enables communication between the cell and its external environment. An additional protective layer *which* provides structural support **is called** <u>the cell wall. The mitochondria</u> are responsible for cellular respiration. A significant portion of the plant cell's volume **is occupied** by <u>the vacuole</u> *which* **is involved** in storing water and providing structural support to the plant. <u>The chloroplast</u> plays a crucial role in photosynthesis.	*which:* refers to things, adds information **passive voice** often used in scientific writing, for example: is/are filled, is/are enclosed

Figure 6.12 The exemplar text explicitly models what should be included in the response and how it should be composed linguistically.

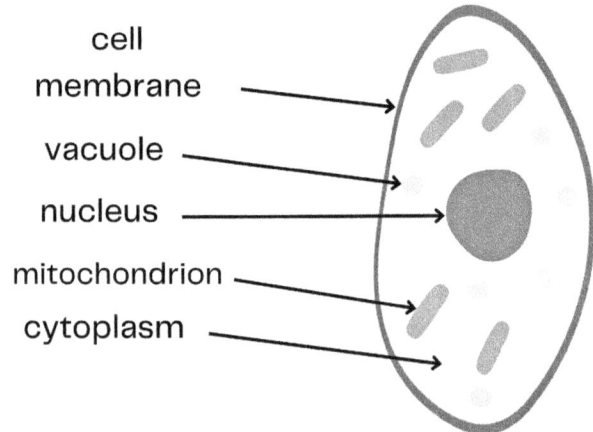

Figure 6.13 A retrieval task preparing students for the main writing stage.

Figure 6.14

explain: what is an animal cell? list: all the key elements	The _____ _____ is a fundamental unit of _____. The _____ _____ _____ a _____, _____, _____, _____, _____. At the core of the _____ _____ lies _____, which _____.	**comprises:** made up of, consists of
name: 1 element and explain its function	The cell's interior **is filled** with the _____, which _____. The animal cell _____ _____ by the cell membrane which provides structural integrity. It also enables _____ _____. The mitochondria _____ _____. Animal cells may contain small _____ _____ _____ _____ in processes such as _____ or _____.	**which:** refers to things, adds information **passive voice** often used in scientific writing, for example: is/are filled, is/are enclosed

Figure 6.14 A language scaffold in the form of a writing frame could be provided. Students may also wish to refer to the model introduced earlier.

Summary

Why?

Parallel writing:

- highlights and emphasises key grammatical structures.
- facilitates the analysis of language relevant to a specific type of writing.
- Introduces patterns and enables controlled use of language.

How?

1. explain the purpose, audience and expectations of the task.
2. plan for an information retrieval task (independent work) and allow the students to discuss the topic (paired or shared discussion) or present the necessary information for completing the task.
3. provide and read aloud a model text, while explaining its organisational and linguistic features (for example vocabulary choices, sentence structure, tenses, use of transitional words, etc.).
4. provide information or prepare an activity where learners can note down key points needed for the writing task.
5. create opportunities for learners to practise and rehearse their answers in pairs, groups or on the class forum.
6. monitor the writing process and provide support, such as sentence starters and instant feedback.

7. allow students to reflect on their writing task by providing an opportunity for them to comment on the content and use metalanguage to discuss key linguistic features they used.

Levels

A-E:

- key words are provided.
- tasks can be completed independently or in pairs/groups.
- sentence stems are provided to support learners in constructing their sentences.
- visuals are provided to aid comprehension.

Dictation activities

Dictation tasks are simple and **easy to implement yet very powerful and effective activities** which can be used across many subjects. They involve listening to a short spoken text and transcribing or writing it down. They allow learners to improve their listening and writing skills whilst focusing on a salient grammatical structure and vocabulary associated with a particular genre or type of writing. The activity can be used at the end of a lesson or unit to review and reinforce grammatical points and key vocabulary or at the very beginning to introduce relevant phrases, idiomatic expressions or new terminology. Dictation is a versatile technique and can be adapted to suit learners' language proficiency levels. It is important though to ensure that an activity of dictating sentences is, apart from centred around a theme or topic of the lesson, planned to spotlight a particular grammatical structure (for example the use of passive voice, the regular and irregular verbs in the past simple tense, modal verbs, prepositions, articles, etc.). Guiding students through the process of identifying and analysing key structures in a meaningful context can develop a deeper understanding of the rules and patterns of the language (Ellis, 2002; Larsen-Freeman, 2014). Guided and independent practice can lead to students' much-increased ability to use these sequences purposefully and accurately in their oral and written responses.

Sentence dictation

Very few secondary school teachers might strongly assert that teaching grammar is a pivotal or regular element in their lessons. Language is a complex and dynamic system characterised by interactions among various linguistic elements. Grammar, in this perspective, is an integral component of language, and its learning is intertwined with other language aspects, such as vocabulary, pronunciation, writing or reading (Larsen-Freeman, 2014). While some linguists and researchers emphasise the significance of students' exposure to language rather than explicit grammar instruction (Krashen, 1988), it is acknowledged that some learners might benefit from a focus on grammar. **Integrating grammar teaching into meaningful tasks** where learners engage in purposeful language use might be the most beneficial approach. Understanding the underlying principles of a grammatical feature can lead to more accurate and comprehensive language acquisition. On the other hand, the importance of implicit learning, which occurs through exposure to meaningful language input and interaction, must not be underestimated. Implicit learning allows learners to develop an intuitive understanding of grammar and use it naturally in a variety of contexts. However, implicit learning might not always lead to accurate usage and can be influenced by various factors (Ellis, 2002).

The example below showcases how grammar can be taught explicitly in a science lesson. There is a strong focus on the form of a studied grammatical structure, the use of the passive voice, but it is done through purposeful and meaningful tasks embedded within the context of the lesson. Students need to be aware that the use of the passive voice makes their writing impartial and objective as it focuses on the process or action being described rather than the person or an object performing the action. Similarly, the use of the passive voice emphasises the importance of data and results instead of the people who conducted the study. Since the use of the passive voice in scientific writing is considered standard practice, the students are expected to use it when, for example, writing up scientific experiments. Although the reasons for using the passive voice seem to be quite straightforward, the structure of this particular grammatical structure requires the mastery, or at least knowledge, of many elements:

<u>the verb 'to be'</u> + **verb in past participle (or verb 3)**

The verb 'to be' needs to be conjugated indicating the tense and the person and the correct form of a verb is required for the second part of the structure. The sentence:

I heated the solution for 30 minutes. (active voice)

becomes:

*The solution <u>was</u> **heated** for two minutes. (passive voice)*

Figure 6.15 shows what the same sentence will look like in different aspects.

The solution	is being is has been was will be is going to be can be might have been	heated.

Figure 6.15 Similar information can be conveyed using different grammatical structures.

Constructing the passive voice might be quite challenging for multilingual students as it requires a specific grammar structure which might differ from the ones used in different languages. Apart from the word order which might pose some issues to some learners, students might overgeneralise the rule of adding the -ed ending for regular verbs. There are many commonly used verbs in science which are irregular:

> make – made: The solution **was made** by mixing the two chemicals.
> take – taken: The samples **were taken** from the patient's blood.
> see – seen: Different results **were seen** when the temperature was lowered significantly.

The rules of constructing the passive voice can be explained and modelled explicitly. It is important to provide plenty of opportunities for exposure and practice so that students can develop their understanding and use of the passive voice.

The examples below illustrate how a grammar dictation technique can be used in mainstream lessons. The students might do an experiment or look at the pictures. Independently, in pairs or groups they are asked to explain what the experiment entailed. At this stage it is very likely that students will use the active voice to describe what they did, for example: *We prepared a solution*. The teacher can then read out the sentences using the passive voice one at a time, either in a sequential or random order. The students write them down under each picture.

1. A solution of 10 ml water and 5 grams of salt was prepared.
2. The solution was stirred for five minutes to dissolve the salt.
3. A piece of potato was placed in the solution and left for 30 minutes.
4. After 30 minutes, the potato was removed from the solution and its weight was recorded.
5. The potato was found to have gained 2 grams in weight.
6. Water from the solution was absorbed.

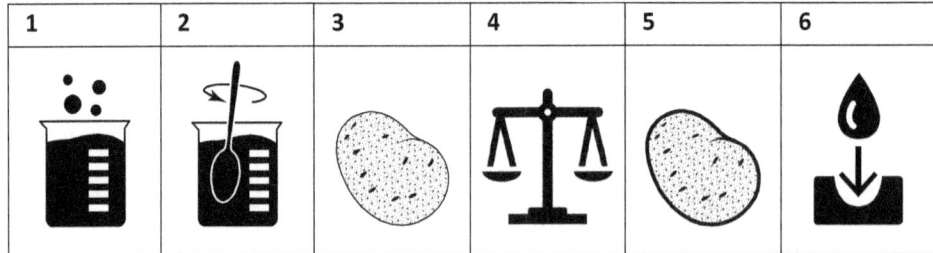

Figure 6.16 Incorporating visual aids supports multilingual learners in grasping the meaning of important words and understanding the sequences of a process.

Once the students have finished writing the sentences, it would be a good idea to discuss the passive voice construction and the reasons for using it. The students could also compare and contrast their own sentences, written either in the active or passive voice, and comment on the syntax.

The activity can be easily adapted for students who are at different levels of English proficiency. Leaving two gaps in each sentence indicates the number of words missing and highlights the two elements of the passive voice. The learners are still exposed to the content and academic language but are asked to focus on a key linguistic feature of this particular type of text.

> A solution of 10 ml water and 5 grams of salt _____ _____ .
> The solution _____ _____ for 5 minutes to dissolve the salt.
> A piece of potato _____ in the solution and _____ for 30 minutes.
> After 30 minutes, the potato _____ from the solution and its weight _____ .
> The potato _____ to have gained 2 grams in weight.
> Water from the solution _____ .

These stages of the activity are heavily focused on language drills. The students should be given an opportunity for independent practice – writing up another experiment would be a good way to check to what degree the learners have understood and are able to use the passive voice in scientific writing.

Transformation dictation

Another, much more challenging, variation of a dictation activity is transformation dictation. The students are tasked with changing the sentences read by the teacher, in this case from active to passive voice. The teacher reads the sentence:

> I filled a glass jar with 100 ml of water.

The students write down its transformation:

> A glass jar was filled with 100 ml of water.

Alternatively, the students could be provided with pictures they have to describe or the sentences written down in the active voice which have to be transformed into the passive voice.

Sentence transformations (either orally or in writing) could be used in many subjects: they provide an excellent opportunity to develop, check or reinforce the students' knowledge of the studied topics and the language simultaneously. The task in Figures 6.17 and 6.18 tests students' ability to recall the information on the Black Death. The sentences in the left-hand

'One to bring them all'

Present tense	Past tense
The Black Death, also known as _____, is a deadly disease that **sweeps** through Europe in the _____ century.	
Its origins **are** traced back to Asia, specifically _____ where it **originates** in the _____.	
The disease **is** spread by fleas that **live** on _____ and **is** transmitted through _____.	
Symptoms of the disease include _____, _____ and _____.	

Figure 6.17 A gap-filling exercise encourages students to recall essential information and practise transforming grammatical structures.

Present tense	Past tense
The Black Death, also known as _____, is a deadly disease that **sweeps** through Europe in the _____ century.	The Black Death, also known as the bubonic plague, was a deadly disease that swept through Europe in the 14th century.
Its origins **are** traced back to Asia, specifically _____ where it **originates** in the _____.	Its origins were traced back to Asia, specifically China where it originates in the 1330s.
The disease **is** spread by fleas that **live** on _____ and **is** transmitted through _____.	The disease was spread by fleas that lived on rats and was transmitted through bites.
Symptoms of the disease include _____, _____ and _____.	Symptoms of the disease include chills, muscle aches and buboes.

Figure 6.18 A completed example of a gap-filling exercise.

column are written in the present tense and there is factual information missing. The students are asked to complete the sentences with the appropriate words, dates and names as well as transform the sentences into the past tense.

Sentence transformation improves the students' **understanding of sentence structures** and enables them to express their ideas in a variety of ways. The students need to analyse the original sentence and manipulate parts of it to convey a very similar meaning. This can be focused on grammatical points as well as vocabulary. One of the most straightforward yet highly effective tasks is rewriting sentences or short paragraphs using Tier 2, academic lexis. The learners could also be asked to reflect on the meaning of the sentences and the potential change: focus on denotations and connotations reflected within the choice of words.

Dictogloss

As subject knowledge is realised through language, we must perceive the two domains as interdependent rather than as two distinct areas existing in parallel. Similarly, there is a natural interrelation among all four skills: speaking, listening, reading and writing. Moreover, in authentic situations, some of these skills are employed simultaneously, while others follow a sequential pattern. Dictogloss is an **integrative approach to practising the four skills**, with an explicit focus on vocabulary and grammatical structures through students' active engagement with the content. Collaboration and purposeful engagement are additional contributing factors to the effectiveness of this task. With a shared goal, learners can clearly perceive it as a meaningful application and extension of their skills.

This activity does not require onerous preparation and can be seamlessly incorporated into any stage of a lesson. Moreover, it can be easily adapted to a variety of English proficiency levels, so that even students who are beginners in acquiring the English language can be exposed to and actively participate in challenging and level-appropriate learning.

The theme of the text, as well as its linguistic components, is crucial to the success of the task. It is advisable to choose a short extract (five to ten sentences, although this can be adapted to suit the profile of the learners) that deals with a familiar subject matter (to avoid confusion and misconceptions). Carefully selecting and explicitly referring to particular grammatical structures and features of a chosen genre are of equal importance. The teacher might decide to draw students' attention, for example, to the passive voice construction used in science as a preferred way to objectively present information, or noun phrases and nominalisation as methods of referring to facts succinctly.

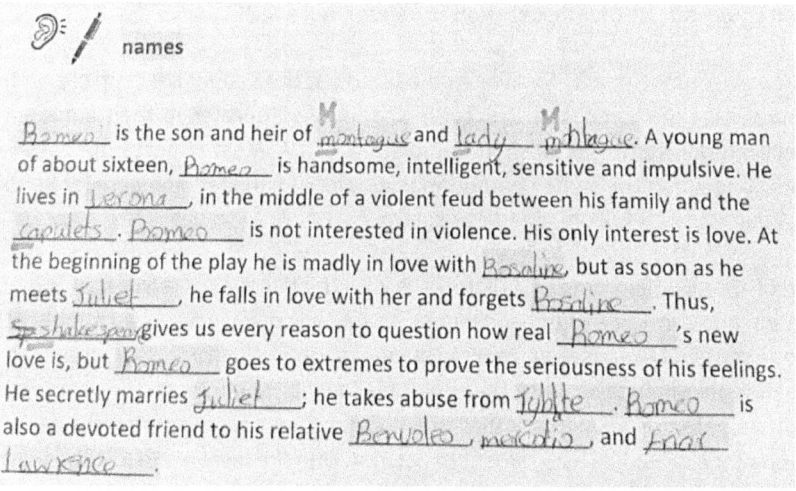

Figure 6.19 Dictogloss can be easily adapted to support learners at different levels.

116 'One to bring them all'

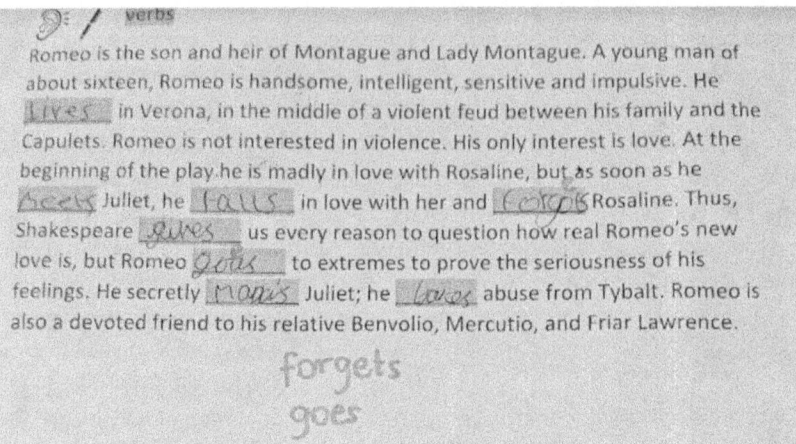

Figure 6.20 Thanks to dictogloss we can focus on key grammatical items.

There are many ways in which dictogloss can be adapted to suit students' current language levels. In the example in Figure 6.19, a group of students identified as B (Early Acquisition) and C (Developing Competence) were given copies of a text from which certain words were deleted. Firstly, they were asked to write the names of the characters with a focus on correct spelling and capital letters.

Next, the correct forms of the present simple tense in third person singular verbs were the focal point of the exercise (Figure 6.20).

Ultimately, the learners were instructed not to refer to the printed texts but to listen to the sentence being read aloud by the teacher once again, take notes independently, discuss them and co-construct the final version in pairs (Figure 6.21).

Since the subject matter was familiar to the learners, they could concentrate on the grammatical accuracy of the chosen structures and, if needed, refer to their knowledge about the main protagonists to successfully complete the task. Most importantly, they were able to actively engage in the same content-appropriate and challenging activity as the rest of the class but with carefully mapped-out scaffolds.

The use of visuals, diagrams and pictures is an effective way to structure the presented information and provide additional support. Visual aids also serve as a springboard during knowledge retrieval exercises and a simple annotation of a picture or diagram can be completed before the main task. Since the content is familiar to students, they can also attempt to anticipate potential vocabulary that they expect to encounter during the task. This is a natural point for formative assessment to occur during the lesson and to enhance students' planning and writing skills. They are encouraged to provide notes and phrases before progressing to sentences.

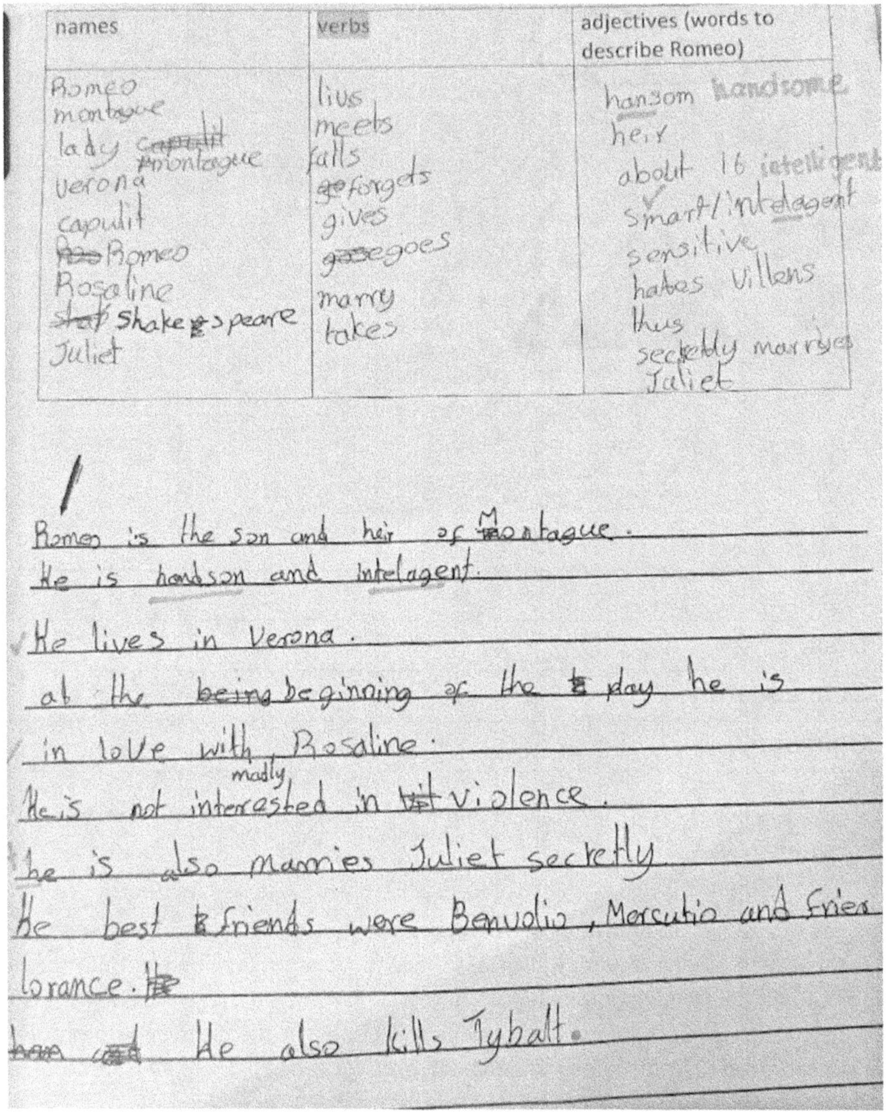

names	verbs	adjectives (words to describe Romeo)
Romeo montague lady montague verona capulit Romeo Rosaline Shakespeare Juliet	livs meets falls forgets gives goes marry takes	hansom handsome heir about 16 intelligent smart/intelagent sensitive hates villens thus seckretly marries Juliet

Romeo is the son and heir of Montague.
He is handson and intelagent.
He lives in Verona.
at the beginning of the day he is in love with Rosaline.
He is not madly interested in violence.
he is also marries Juliet seckretly
He best friends were Benvolio, Mercutio and Frier Lorance.
He also kills Tybalt.

Figure 6.21 Dictogloss can be used with students at all levels of English language acquisition.

In this specific example in Figure 6.22, there is a clear focus on cohesive devices (linking words that outline a sequence of events) as they are provided as sentence starters. This layout and linguistic scaffold would be suitable for students identified at levels A and B. It would also be beneficial for those at higher levels, as the teacher can expertly model and explain the paragraph structures that can be employed in similar tasks.

118 'One to bring them all'

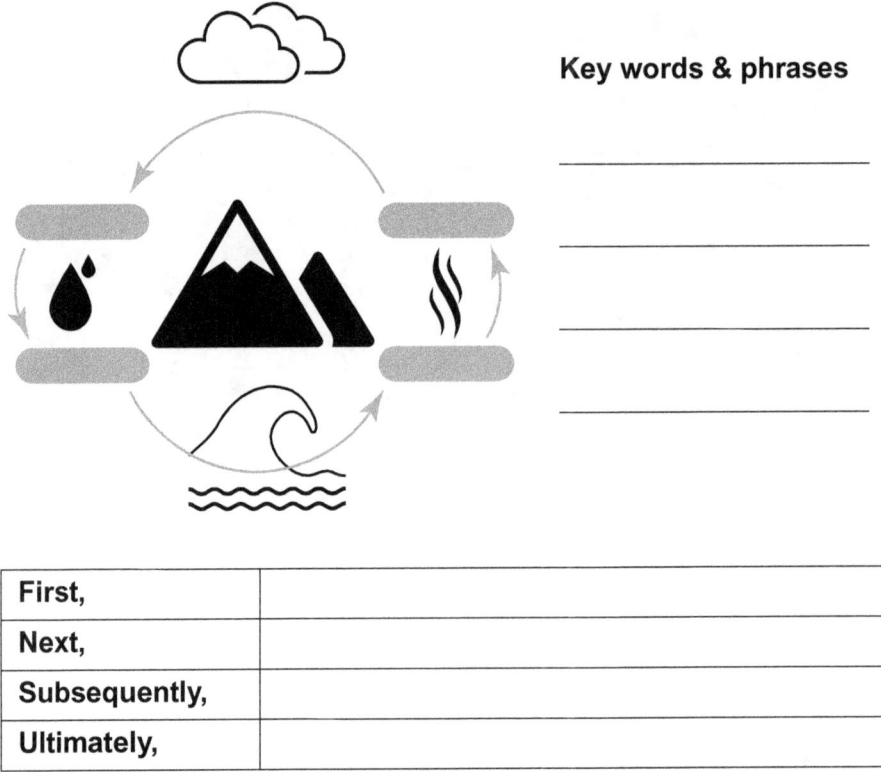

Figure 6.22 It is beneficial if particular grammatical structures are highlighted during dictation tasks.

Dictogloss is **a dynamic and interactive approach** that encourages active engagement and collaboration among learners. It offers a holistic way to **develop multiple language skills** in an integrated manner. The length of a text chosen, the number of times it is read and the type and level of scaffolding provided, depends on the class and its profile, but there are certain steps which need to be undertaken for the activity to be a successful and effective one.

1. select a text which is based around the topic your students have been studying. It can be a short paragraph, a dialogue or a narrative. Decide which grammatical structures, words and phrases or features of the genre are going to be the main focus.
2. read the text to your students at a natural pace. During this phase, students should focus on understanding the general meaning of the text without capturing every word.
3. after listening to the text, students individually take notes on key points, important vocabulary and sentence structure they remember. Encourage them to focus on the main ideas and the overall flow of the text.

4. students work in pairs or groups to reconstruct the text based on their notes. The goal is to capture the essence of the text while maintaining accurate grammar and vocabulary usage.
5. each pair or group is encouraged to discuss and make decisions regarding word choices, sentence structure and overall coherence.
6. read aloud or provide a written version of the original text so that students can compare their texts with the original. This step encourages reflection and highlights areas for improvement.
7. together with your class discuss specific grammatical structures, vocabulary choices and sentence organisation. This is an opportunity to explain any linguistic concepts that may arise.

The template in Figure 6.23 can be used to clearly outline each step of the activity. Students could also be promoted to concentrate on specific elements of the text, such as noun/noun phrases and verbs.

Summary

Why?

Dictation activities:

- expose learners to authentic language input, helping develop their listening and comprehension skills.
- reinforce the understanding of sentence structure, verb tenses, word order and other grammatical elements.
- students encounter and practise words and phrases in context and experience how different linguistic elements work together in a coherent context.
- focus on key grammatical patterns can promote cross-linguistic awareness.
- if conducted in pairs and groups, promote collaboration and interaction between peers which enhance both linguistic and social skills.
- can be easily adapted to suit learners of different language proficiency levels.
- highlight and amplify the features of different genres and subgenres.
- encourage learners to take an active role in reconstructing the text and making linguistic decisions.
- allow for explicit grammar instruction in a meaningful and engaging context.
- involve four skills of listening, speaking, reading and writing.

How?

1. students need to be familiar with the topic of the text.
2. grammatical structures or key vocabulary, which are characteristic of the task, need to be highlighted and/or explicitly explained to students.
3. students need to be actively participating in the collaborative learning process working either in pairs or small groups.

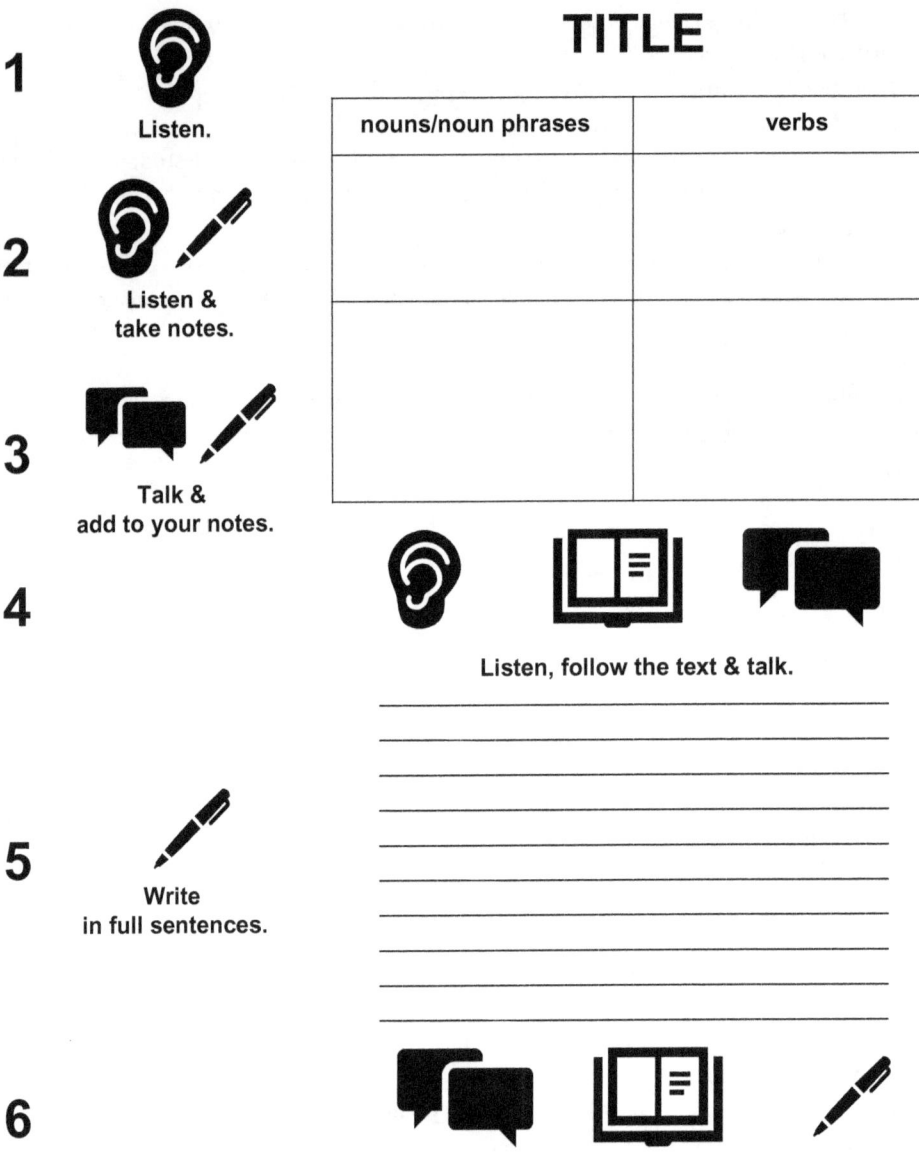

Figure 6.23 Using a template with visuals can assist students in comprehending and completing each step of a dictation activity.

Levels

A-E:

- key words, sentence stems, visuals provided.
- completed independently or in pairs/groups.
- varying length of texts used.
- the number of times the text is read could be altered to suit the profile of the class.

Routines and habits aka sentence starters and frames

You are a specialist in your field, whether it is mathematics, history, science or music. You possess a high level of knowledge and expertise. Now, imagine that you have to deliver a lesson in a different language. Perhaps you are new to this language, or maybe you have a rudimentary understanding of a few expressions and perhaps you can engage in a casual conversation in that language. The question arises: would you be able to deliver a high-quality session in a different language, even though you have a comprehensive grasp of the content? While a few individuals might manage this feat, many would not.

Many EAL learners, including those who are new to English, often possess cognitive abilities that far surpass their linguistic competencies. These students may bring a wealth of knowledge, skills and creativity to the learning environment. However, their linguistic proficiency in English might not yet fully reflect their intellectual potential. **Prefabricated routines**, which are memorised phrases or sentences as well as prefabricated patterns, which are partly fixed and partly creative units are very pragmatic tools to allow multilingual learners to take part in interactions in lessons (Krashen, 1988). If a new student joins your lesson and they are in the early stages of acquiring English, neither of you would be comfortable with simply allowing the language acquisition process to take its time. If a child is in your lesson and you are comparing and contrasting animal and plant cells, it would be extremely beneficial to provide prefabricated patterns, known as sentence starters so that the students can take part in the lesson. At this stage, the student does not have to understand every integral element of the phrase: 'On the other hand, _____ as long as they can articulate their science knowledge. Similarly, prefabricated routines, for example: I don't agree with this statement' need not be analysed with respect to the use of negation in the present simple tense for the first person. At this stage, students can read and with time memorise the whole phrases to express their opinions.

comparing	**contrasting**
Similarly, _____.	• However, _____.
Likewise, _____.	• In contrast _____.
Both ____ and ____	• In comparison _____.
Not only ____ but also ____	• On the other hand, _____.
Neither ____ nor ____	• ____ while ____.
____ and ____ are alike ____	• ____ whereas ____
____ is similar to ____	• ____ differs from ____.
cause-effect	**additional ideas**
____ results from ____.	Also, ____
____ is the result of ____.	Furthermore ____.
Due to ____.	In addition, ____.
Because of ____.	Moreover, ____.
____ is the consequence of ____.	Additionally, ____.
As a result of ____.	Another (+noun) ____.
As a consequence of ____.	An additional (+noun) ____.
making a connection	**asking for clarification**
This is similar to ____.	Do you mean ____?
This is different from ____.	Could you give an example?
This photograph/strategy/painting reminds me of ____.	Can you clarify this point/statement?
I can relate to ____ because ____.	Could you elaborate on that, please?
It is interesting that ____.	Can you say it differently?

Figure 6.24 Sentence starters are invaluable tools for EAL learners as they provide a foundation for expressing their thoughts and ideas effectively in English.

expressing opinions	predicting
I strongly believe that _____.	I predict that _____.
Personally, I think _____.	If _____ then _____.
In my opinion _____.	The illustration/diagram shows that _____
As far as I'm concerned _____.	so I predict _____.
I am of the opinion that _____.	I can use my background knowledge to predict that _____.
	Based on the fact that __ I predict that __.
agreeing/disagreeing	sequencing ideas
I agree with you because _____.	Firstly, _____. Secondly, _____.
To add on to what __ was saying about __.	Thirdly, _____.
In addition I think that __.	First of all _____.
That's a valid point because _____.	Then _____. Next, _____.
I disagree with you because _____.	Lastly, _____
I partly agree with you but _____.	Finally, _____.
I can see why you would say __ but have you thought about _____?	Previously, _____.
Have you considered _____?	Meanwhile, _____
	Gradually _____.

Figure 6.24 Contd.

Sentence starters can be used during speaking, rehearsal activities and consequently in writing. Similarly, speaking frames for longer and more complex explanations can transition into writing frames used for essays and reports. Typically, sentence starters and speaking or writing frames are used with A–C students but they can be easily adjusted to ensure that all students, regardless of their English language proficiency levels, can practise academic talk or writing in a structured and supportive way.

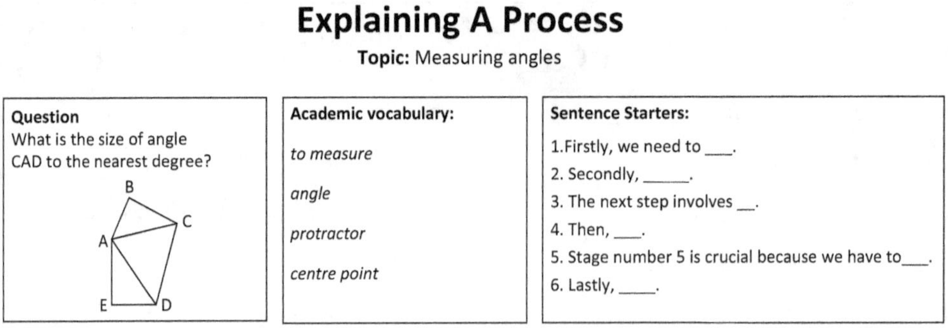

Explaining A Process
Topic: Measuring angles

Question	Academic vocabulary:	Sentence Starters:
What is the size of angle CAD to the nearest degree?	to measure	1. Firstly, we need to ___.
	angle	2. Secondly, ___.
	protractor	3. The next step involves ___.
	centre point	4. Then, ___.
		5. Stage number 5 is crucial because we have to___.
		6. Lastly, ___.

Figure 6.25 Combining the content and linguistic components of lessons using sentence starters creates a supportive environment for EAL learners.

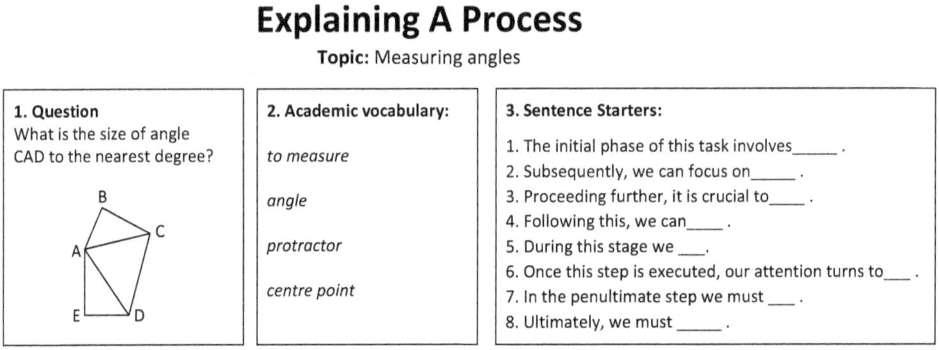

Explaining A Process
Topic: Measuring angles

1. Question	2. Academic vocabulary:	3. Sentence Starters:
What is the size of angle CAD to the nearest degree?	to measure	1. The initial phase of this task involves ___.
	angle	2. Subsequently, we can focus on ___.
	protractor	3. Proceeding further, it is crucial to ___.
	centre point	4. Following this, we can ___.
		5. During this stage we ___.
		6. Once this step is executed, our attention turns to ___.
		7. In the penultimate step we must ___.
		8. Ultimately, we must ___.

Figure 6.26 Speaking and writing frames allow for the adjustment of linguistic complexity.

The second example involves the same lesson content but is significantly more complex in terms of the language used to express ideas sequentially. Students could also be prompted with questions like, 'What are you planning to do? What have you accomplished so far? How did you solve it?' Notice that their responses would need to consider the questions and their associated grammar, resulting in answers such as 'I'm going to draw a triangle. I have drawn a triangle. I drew a triangle'.

As students' proficiency develops, the scaffolding of sentence starters and speaking/writing frames should be gradually removed and used judiciously in the later stages, ensuring that students turn to a more creative use of language rather than relying on prefabricated phrases.

Summary

Why?

Sentence starters, speaking/writing frames:

- support language development as they provide scaffolding for EAL students to express themselves effectively.
- build confidence by offering a structured starting point for communication.
- encourage active participation in class discussions and written tasks.
- enhance the clarity of communication by facilitating coherent expression.

How?

1. you might want to start with simple sentence starters and frames, gradually increasing complexity as students progress.
2. align the starters and frames with the lesson's content to support comprehension.
3. use visuals or charts to accompany sentence starters to enhance understanding.
4. provide constructive feedback on language use to foster improvement.

Levels

A-E:

- particularly beneficial to students at A–C levels.
- can be tailored to suit students at various proficiency levels.
- should be treated as a scaffold, not a permanent feature in our lessons.

References

Cameron, L. 2003. *Writing in English as an Additional Language at Key Stage 4 and post-16.* [Online] Accessed 25 February 2023. Available from: www.naldic.org.uk.

Cummins, J. 1984. *Bilingualism and Special Education: Issues in Assessment and Pedagogy.* Clevedon: Multilingual Matters.

Cummins, J. 2021. *Rethinking the Education of Multilingual Students.* Bristol: Multilingual Matters.

Derewianka, B. and Jones, P. 2016. *Teaching Language in Context.* Melbourne: Oxford University Press.

Ellis, R. 2002. Grammar Teaching – Practice or Consciousness-Raising? In J. Richards and W. Renandya, eds. *Methodology in Language Teaching: An Anthology of Current Practice.* Cambridge: Cambridge University Press, pp. 167–174.

Gibbons, P. 2015. *Scaffolding Language, Scaffolding Learning: Teaching Second Language Learners in the Mainstream Classroom.* Portsmouth: Heinemann.

Harmer, J. 1997. *Teaching and Learning Grammar.* New York: Longman.

Harmer, J. 2004. *How to Teach Writing*. Harlow: Pearson Education Limited.

Hyland, K. 2003. *Second Language Writing*. Cambridge: Cambridge University Press.

Krashen, S. D. 1988. *Second Language Acquisition and Second Language Learning*. Exeter: Prentice Hall International.

Larsen-Freeman, D. 2014. Teaching Grammar. In M. Celce-Murcia, D. M. Brinton and M. A. Snow, eds. *Teaching English as a Second or Foreign Language*. Boston, MA: Heinle/Cengage Learning, pp. 256-270.

Lemov, D. 2021. *Teach Like a Champion 3.0: 63 Techniques that Put Students on the Path to College*. Hoboken: Jossey Bass.

Sharples, R. 2021. *Teaching EAL: Evidence-Based Strategies for Classroom and School*. Bristol: Multilingual Matters.

Thornbury, S. 2006. *An A-Z of ELT. A Dictionary of Terms and Concepts*. Oxford: Macmillan Education.

Wong Filmore, L. 2009. *English Language Development: Acquiring the Language Needed for Literacy and Learning*. [Online] Accessed 4 October 2023. Available from: http://assets.pearsonschool.com/asset_mgr/current/201010/English%20Language%20Development.pdf.

CONCLUSION

As you walk along, you suddenly notice the face of a young man approaching you, and there is something very familiar about him. He reaches you with a warm smile and says, 'Good morning, Miss!' It is then that you recognise him as Adam, a student from your geography class. He has grown much taller, his hairstyle has changed and he must be in his early twenties now. You discover that he is very soon graduating from university with a degree in business management. It surprises you, as you had expected him to pursue a career in geography given his impressive GCSE results. Playfully, you feel an urge to tell him off for veering away from geography. Just as you are about to do it, Adam turns to a woman a few metres away and says something in Tigrinya. 'It's my mum', Adam explains, 'I need to go, Miss. Thank you'.

Drawing upon my 15 years of experience working with EAL and multilingual learners, I have had the privilege of witnessing countless inspiring journeys, much like that of Adam. Adam's story, like so many others, demonstrates that while we may start our journeys at different points, we all possess the innate potential to contribute and develop. The realisation of the immense potential inherent in every individual hinges upon the unwavering commitment of all educators. It is our responsibility as teachers to foster a nurturing and inclusive environment within our classroom, one where all students can flourish academically.

In such a conducive atmosphere, students should be both challenged and supported in their academic pursuits, facilitating their holistic growth and personal development. *Empowering EAL Learners in Secondary Schools: A Practical Resources to Support the Language Development of Multilingual Learners* emphasises the vital importance of inclusion, a sense of belonging and a pursuit of academic excellence for all multilingual students. These students enrich our classrooms and communities with their unique perspective, culture and experiences.

Together, we can create a more inclusive and equitable educational landscape for all students, setting them on a path to soar just like Adam and countless others who have found their wings.

DOI: 10.4324/9781003386810-7

INDEX

additive bilingualism 2-3

behaviourism 14, 16
BICS 21-22, 23, 95

CALP 22-23, 95
cognates 32
cohesion 71-73
collocations 47-51
comprehensible input 79
connectionist theory 15
'critical period' 17
Cummins, J. 20, 24
CUP 13, 64

dictation activities: dictogloss 115-121; sentence dictation 110-113; transformation 113-114

EAL 1-2
easification 79-83, 81, 88-89, 92-93
English language proficiency levels 20-21, 23
ESL 1

Frayer model 41-44

graphic organisers 66, 100-104

homonyms 32

innatism 14, 16
input theory 17
interactionism 14

Krashen, S. 17, 79, 121

language 4-5; heritage language 5

multilingualism 1, 7

parallel writing 104; sentence writing 104-105; paragraph writing 105-110

sentence starters 121-125
sequential bilingualism 4
simplification 79-83, 87-88, 91-92
simultaneous bilingualism 4
substitution tables 96-100
subtractive bilingualism 3-4

text engineering *see* easification

usage based theory 16

visuals 73, 76-77
vocabulary teaching: tier 1 30, 33-37, 44-45; tier 2 30, 31, 36-40, 44-5; tier 3 30, 40-42, 44-45
Vygotsky 15

word cards 34-36

For Product Safety Concerns and Information please contact our EU
representative GPSR@taylorandfrancis.com
Taylor & Francis Verlag GmbH, Kaufingerstraße 24, 80331 München, Germany

www.ingramcontent.com/pod-product-compliance
Lightning Source LLC
Chambersburg PA
CBHW082101230426
43670CB00017B/2917